Do you know the meaning of this sentence?
Alter est, ergo sum.
(answer within, p.40)

T0368206

ON BEING ALONE:

I exist because others exist. If I do not exist, how can I see them and know that they are different from me? They confirm me and give me identity. If I had been born on a desert island on which my mother and I were the only creatures, and if my mother were swept away on a wave, my cries to Heaven would not be heard and I would pass silently into the void. To be alone is not to be. (Preface)

RELATIONSHIP:

To understand a relationship we are obliged to understand the series of interactions that are its building-blocks. The sum of the interactions that a person has experienced with another defines a relationship, and the sum of the relationships that the person has experienced defines a life. (p.42)

EMPATHY:

The ability to empathize can be learned by the tenth year of life and remains a lifelong trait. It is noticeably missing in psychopaths, sociopaths, and sadists of any stripe. When present, it will leaven and enlighten any disagreement between people, because it shows a willingness, as they say, to wear the other person's shoes and see life through another's eyes. Here is the Golden

Rule in practical terms. An empathic bond is the finest expression of relationship. (p.153)

DEATH:

Death teaches life everything. When I wrote that, in *The Meaning of Life*, I meant it literally, because we cannot see life plainly without contemplating its negation—life's reciprocal. In that context, death gives a value for life: the specter of death, looming before each of us every day, leads us to cherish what we have, in peril of losing it. If death did not exist, we would have to invent it. (p.94)

LIFE:

If you can give to a relationship more than you take from it, even more that it asks of you, you will meet every expectation that life has for you. The reason we are on this planet is to establish, maintain, enjoy, and fulfill relationships. In this view, relationship is not everything. It is the only thing. (p.36)

LIFE
IS
RELATIONSHIP

LIFE
IS
RELATIONSHIP

Louis Everstine

Library of Congress Control Number: 2005906601
ISBN: Hardcover   978-1-5992-6205-5
               Softcover   978-1-5992-6204-8

This book was printed in the United States of America.

Cover image: "The Cathedral" by Auguste Rodin

Photograph of the author: Cynthia P. Larson

Text preparation: Rana Kim

Production assistance: Aimee Aborque

To order additional copies of this book, contact:
Xlibris Corporation
1-888-795-4274
www.Xlibris.com
Orders@Xlibris.com
29686

CONTENTS

For Aden, my father,
the finest man I have ever known

PREFACE

Early in Autumn, 1960, I arrived in Cambridge, England, to enroll in the University as a graduate student in Philosophy and become a member of Fitzwilliam House (now College). A month before, I had competed a doctoral dissertation in Clinical Psychology in the States, and this was my first visit to another country. In Cambridge at the time, Philosophy was called "Moral Sciences," and a few weeks after arriving I was invited to join the Moral Sciences Club, comprised of students and faculty (called "Dons").

The first Club meeting that I attended was held in the rooms of Richard Braithwaite, a Don, in King's College. The meeting agenda was invariably a paper read by a Cambridge faculty member or someone brought in from another University such as Oxford or London or Manchester; there would be questions and sherry and refreshments after the talk. At that first meeting, Braithwaite drew me aside and whispered, conspiratorially, "You see that chair? That's where Wittgenstein sat when he demolished Popper." He was confiding in me about a meeting that occurred in 1946, when there had been a debate between Ludwig Wittgenstein, then a Cambridge professor, and Karl Popper, a philosopher of much renown from the London School of Economics, who had been asked to present a paper for the delectation of the Club (This incident is the subject of a recent book by Edmonds and Eidinow, *Wittgenstein's Poker*; the title refers to a poker from Braithwaite's fireplace that Wittgenstein was handling in an idly menacing way, using it as a sort of baton to emphasize his points.) Suffice it to say that the Popper-Wittgenstein debate was not soon forgotten, and that the ghost of Wittgenstein haunts Cambridge still.

After Wittgenstein, the ship of Philosophy, lacking its guru whose ideas could dazzle even if they couldn't enlighten, foundered. The titles of some contemporary papers tell the story of this era of intellectual stagnation: "Word and Object," "Matter and Consciousness," and my favorite, Thomas Nagel's "What Is It Like to Be a Bat?" With time and with more exposure to the Moral Sciences Club, I realized that Philosophy at Cambridge was not at all scientific and had very little to do with morals. This was not the least of the curiosities that I encountered during my four years of study in England (the first at Cambridge, followed by three years at

Oxford). Many a time I thought of those lyrics by W. S. Gilbert that go:

> Things are seldom what they seem,
> Skim milk masquerades as cream.
> Highlows pass in patent leathers,
> Jackdaws strut in peacock's feathers.
> ("H.M.S. Pinafore")

Now that I look back on my journey to England, the Holy See of fundamentalist Philosophy, I most regret its self-delusion. How could wise men have formed the impression that any element of their work might benefit mankind in any way?

I moved on to the University of California at Berkeley and continued my studies in Philosophy, but there, too, the discipline was focused on answering questions such as "How do I know what another person is thinking?," or the ultimate conundrum, "How do I know what I am thinking?" There seemed to be no end to the self-referential nature of the inquiries of these scholars, and the path that they followed had no foreseeable destination.

I opened a private practice of Clinical Psychology, and for thirty years have done my best to help people solve their problems. Occasionally, a family that had lost a loved-one to suicide asked me to meet with the surviving family members to help them cope with their tragedy. Naturally, only the passage of time will truly help, but in my encounters with them I was struck by the power of their anguish and shame. The death of a loved-one often had, in addition, brought to the surface the family's web of secret alliances and animosities, and the cohesion of the family was often torn apart. I knew that suicide is a willed action, not the result of accident or whim, and I began to ask what the motive of the suicidal person might be. The answer lies in the effect it produces, namely the punishment of the person's family or a family member or some other person of significance, such as a loved-one or close friend. In short, a person kills himself or herself to destroy a relationship.

What I learned from this observation is that people stay alive because of relationships, usually one in particular, and that to prevent suicide requires that at least one relationship is healthy and fulfilling. I wrote two books to propose methods for fostering healthy relationships, one for therapists and one for non-professionals whose friend or loved-one has made suicidal threats. A therapist must treat the crucial relationship, not just the threatener. The friend must convince the threatener that he or she belongs to one relationship that is worth living for.

Far beyond pursuing the goal of preventing suicide, and indeed beyond my role as a psychologist, I began to take stock of what I had learned about life from an understanding of death. If willful death is the product of a failed relationship and relationship can preserve life, an ancient secret is revealed and a primordial truth affirmed. We live because of others.

I recalled my sojourn in the Wonderland of Philosophy, and found a question left unanswered: how is it possible to have a Philosophy that is not a Moral Philosophy? And since I had come this far, I couldn't ignore another question: how it is possible to have a Moral Philosophy without knowing the meaning of life? And because knowing it is only the first station in a rite of passage, how is it possible to know the meaning of life and not live in accord with it day after day?

This book is the natural extension of another book of mine, *The Meaning of Life* (2000), that defines human existence in relationship terms. I exist because others exist. If I do not exist, how can I see them and know that they are different from me? They confirm me and give me identity. If I had been born on a desert island on which my mother and I were the only creatures, and if my mother were swept away on a wave, my cries to Heaven would not be heard and I would pass silently into the void. To be alone is not to be.

Saint Paul de Vence
20 August 2003

ACKNOWLEDGMENTS

My idea of a Philosopher was Oliver Reiser. A Professor for many years at the University of Pittsburgh, Reiser was a passionate seeker of truth. He thought of himself as a Cosmologist, and much of his writing attempted to lead the reader to an understanding of what that discipline means and where it leads. For me, it was not what Reiser said in his lectures, but that he believed in it so fervently. I don't recall a word, but I thrilled to the music.

The most charismatic teacher that I met was John Crowe Ransom. Reticent and soft-spoken, he was in every way the Southern gentleman. They came to Kenyon from across the country to sit at his feet—James Wright and Ed Doctorow and Bob Mezey and Anthony Hecht among them. For them and for me, Ransom *was* poetry.

The most flamboyant teacher I knew was Ashley Montagu at The New School. He spoke slowly, every syllable falling trippingly from the tongue. His prim delivery often obscured the weight of his ideas, but the matron ladies of Fifth Avenue loved him like a son.

These were teachers with whom I studied. Others I encountered in books, of whom Freud and Camus and Shaw I am fondest. Their words invited me to the world of ideas that is my daily refuge.

As an exemplar of relationship, I give you mine with Diana, my wife of 32 years. She once asked me what I most wanted to do in life, and I said "write books." And so I have done, with Diana's blessing, and I shall never be able to thank her enough. Soul-mate, confessor, best friend, she is the truest teacher.

PROLOGUE

Doña Ana (crying to the universe): "A father! A father for the Superman!"
—Bernard Shaw, "Man and Superman"

On a crisp Autumn evening, eons ago, the Life Force visited Mother Nature in her grotto, at her invitation. "Come in, my friend," she said, "We don't see enough of each-other."

"Thank you for asking me, but I haven't any idea *why* you asked me."

"All will be revealed in time," said Mother Nature. "But here, let me have that cape. Rest yourself by the fireplace. Have a drink." She took his cape, draped it over a chair, and led him to a loveseat facing the fireplace. She gave him a stone flask with a liquid in it that seemed to bubble and glow, and poured herself one of the same. A lightning stroke down the chimney set the lava rocks in the fireplace aflame. At the sound of thunder, he turned toward the opening of the cavelike room and saw, across the sky outside, an Aurora Borealis. "For your amusement," said Mother Nature.

"I'm flattered. You never cease to amaze me, the wonders you perform. I must confess, I've missed our chats. We're too busy, both of us. Tell me, is there some way I can help?"

"Just hear me out," she replied. "You're my sounding-board. You never give me bad advice. Only now, I need you more than ever."

There was a pause while both stared into the fire. Finally, the Life Force cleared his throat and said "I'm a great admirer of your work. I like what you've done with those protozoa, and . . ." She broke in with "That's it. That's what I want to tell you. I'm thinking of something new. It's risky. It'll change everything. I've never been so scared about putting an idea into practice but . . . it won't go away."

"Ideas have a way of daring you to put them into practice," said her guest. "What is it?"

"Well, what if? . . . what if life forms were divided into two classes or categories or types, and instead of either type being able to reproduce itself—as we have now—the two would have to unite in some way to beget new life?"

"Hold on. 'Beget,' what's that? I don't know that word."

"Of course not. I made it up."

"But what are you saying about two organisms uniting? . . . I'm appalled. It's complicated enough with one . . . Are you trying to make more work for me?"

"Not at all; rather less. Think about it. These one-celled organisms can divide any time, producing new ones that require the spark of life. When two unite to make one, your job will be easier."

"All right. It's true that my role is to imbue with life the creatures you have designed. But where's the advantage here? How could this improve on your life's work? After all, you've had your expanding galaxies and your Big Bangs and your cataclysms and burnt-out suns and continents drifting apart. You achieved all that before I came along—a brilliant career. But now you seem to be stuck on creature-making. This could be the least of your achievements."

"Never mind that. One of my best traits is to reinvent myself. I'm never stale. You said that about me once yourself, remember?: 'Age cannot wither her, nor custom stale her infinite variety.' Ah, but we were inseparable then. Isn't it so?"

The Life Force (blushing): "Ah, youth . . . it's true, we had a lot of fun then. But we never thought of doing what you—what I think you're suggesting."

"Why must you be so coy? You're making my point. If my DNA were combined with yours, imagine what we could create—together."

"And any two similar forms, I take it?"

"Exactly. The gene combinations are astronomical in their complexity."

"Of course, but wait a minute. Let me think about this. Give me another of those drinks." She busied herself about, pouring him another flask of the effervescent brew, which he sipped pensively. "Let's see if I have this straight. Unless two organisms of the same species encounter each-other, experience some attraction to each-other and . . . let's say 'agree,' no procreation will occur and the race will not be perpetuated."

"You always look on the dark side," retorted Mother Nature. "Naturally, the lowest orders will keep on reproducing themselves, like protozoa; I find them boring. But in my new plan, the potential is enormous: when the DNA of one life is merged with the DNA of another, a better creature than both could emerge. The species would improve from one era to the next, perhaps even perfect itself."

They both fell silent for a time. Suddenly, there was a deafening rumbling coming from outside, followed by grinding, screeching sounds. He saw a wall of ice cover the cave opening. It gave him a start and he turned to her for reassurance. "It's nothing, just a glacier. It will be gone soon, what with the Warming."

"Oh, yes, the Warming. Now tell me if I've got my part in this venture. You want to bring creatures together in pairs, and when they make a new creature I reach out with my magic finger and touch it with life."

"That's it exactly."

"Capital," said the Life Force. "It's a hell of an idea. I'm sure there will be times when it doesn't work at all, and a species falls far short of perfecting itself, but it's worth a try . . . Look here, who? . . . How does this thing get started? Where does it begin?"

Mother Nature shook her head. "You are so impatient. Your question will be answered before long. For now, let me offer you a light supper." She took his arm in hers and steered him through a curtain into the next room, where the only light was supplied by tiny candles. There was a low table laden with exotic fruits, meats, and sweet temptations. The only places for sitting were cushions on the floor. Soft music played in the background. When he was seated, the Life Force wore a slightly befuddled look, as though he were trying to make sense of what he had heard. He looked like a man who wasn't quite sure of where he was and how he got there. Then, smiling, as if he knew the answer, he asked "This way of yours—for making new creatures—what shall we call it?"

Mother Nature (laughing): "You may call it whatever you like. I call it sex."

Here we can discreetly draw the curtain. The rest, as they say, is History.

For one human being to love another; that is perhaps the most difficult of all our tasks, the ultimate, the last test and proof, the work for which all other work is but preparation.

—Rainer Maria Rilke, *Letters to a Young Poet*

I

The Meaning of Life

... the meaning of life is the most urgent of questions. How to answer it?
— Albert Camus, *The Myth of Sisyphus*

... a complete theory [of the universe] should in time be understandable in broad principle by everyone, not just a few scientists. Then we shall all, philosophers, scientists and just ordinary people, be able to take part in the discussion of the question of why it is that we and the universe exist. If we find the answer to that, it would be the ultimate triumph of human reason—for then we should know the mind of God.
— Stephen Hawking, *A Brief History of Time*

Most people don't know why they are alive. Most do not even ask the question. They live, and that's enough for them. Many whom they knew have died, and it's those people's misfortune. Living is a privilege, not a right, but too many questions about why could lead to hubris. You keep it as long as you can, and when the lights go out *c'est la vie*. We may, as the end comes, ask "What did it all mean?," but there is no guarantee of an answer. A man might ask why he was born 80 years ago, but the only reply might be, as Camus noted, "the unreasonable silence of the world."

If you ask people what life means, you may be greeted by embarrassment and a shrug of dismissal. They know but they would rather not tell. They don't know but it's not important. They answer with humor or a facetious remark that mocks the question. If they are religious, only their god can answer; at least, all will be revealed on Judgment Day. If he or she is a hedonist, life amounts to the pursuit of pleasure and the avoidance of pain. If one is a soldier, it means honor on the battlefield. If a politician, no one will ever know. For the cynic, "There is no reason for life and life has no meaning" (Somerset Maugham, 1938). For the disheartened, "Life is what happens to us while we are making other plans" (Allen Saunders, 1957). For the optimist, "Life is an ecstasy" (Ralph Waldo Emerson, 1860).

There seems to be no consensus about life's meaning, no firm conclusion nor even a will to find one. This state of affairs begs the psychological question of why people would prefer not to know why they exist. The reason must be locked away in the subconscious because it is too frightening for the ego to acknowledge. A person's ego is the sense of self, and we protect this sense at all costs. The purpose of this book is to supply a definition of life that people will not ignore and can accept.

An earlier book, *The Meaning of Life*, put forth the idea that the meaning of life is relationship. Many have reached this conclusion, but it may not have been given enough importance or sufficiently thought-through. Some things we know, but do not know we know them; other things we know that we know, but we seldom make use of those insights in our daily lives. For these reasons, the significance of the idea as a guiding principle for human values is worth judging. Its utility as a guideline for everyday conduct is worth exploring. Its power to inspire new ethical standards deserves assessment. In short, it is a proposition that cannot be ignored.

The notion that relationship transcends other human values competes with many alternative views, among which are those implying that life's purpose is to:

1. qualify for life everlasting, by proving one's virtue through earthly deeds;
2. reach a high level of achievement in one's chosen field of activity;

3. create a work of art that will draw critical acclaim;

4. acquire wealth, as in the expression "He who dies with the most toys, wins," or when a person's "worth" is attached to a dollar sign;

5. establish a record in a sport;

6. make a scientific discovery;

7. participate in a military victory;

8. win an election, thereby acquiring arbitrary power;

9. invent a product or process that will carry one's name;

10. become the most prominent person in one's family.

There may be many more goals like these that motivate human striving, but most can be traced to one or more of the Seven Deadly Sins. They are the empty prizes bestowed by false gods. They signify nothing.

Life is worth more than any of those delusions. It offers more than the pleasures of the flesh or success or power or being famous or any other tribute to human vanity. It even mocks life for a person to seek immortality, because, without meaning, the person would merely exchange one empty prize for another. No, there is but one life and its meaning lies elsewhere.

Life is not an ideology or a concept or a quest or a preparation or a test. It has nothing to do with, for example:

1. social movements, as for instance the human rights movement, communism, environmentalism, etc;

2. religious teaching of any faith;

3. acquisition of any earthly object or thing; i.e., property of any kind;

4. philanthropy in the sense of giving away a portion of one's worldly goods to assuage the guilt of having them;

5. insurance against death or a guarantee of a second life in some unearthly realm;

6. political abstractions such as freedom. justice, or democracy;

7. honor, bravery, fearlessness, integrity, fortitude, pride, or other vainglorious fantasies.

Shakespeare knew how seductive and how insubstantial are goals such as these when he wrote these lines for Falstaff:

" . . . honor pricks me on. Yea, but how if honor pricks me off when I come on? how then? Can honor set to a leg? no: or an arm? no: or take away the grief of a wound? no. Honor hath no skill in surgery, then? no. What is honor? a word. What is that word, honor? . . . Who hath it? he that died o'Wednesday . . . will it not live with the living? no . . . Therefore I'll have none of it. Honor is a mere scutcheon."

("Henry IV," Part I, Scene I)

The viewpoint of this book is not that the Eternal Verities listed above are worthless, but rather that they are misleading. For example, if we "buy into" the American Dream of fame and fortune, we are not only missing something but are wasting vast periods of our lives on trivia. The system of false values catalogued above encourages people to compete among themselves to be thought-of as:

- the wisest
- the richest
- the best-looking
- the hardest-working
- the brightest
- the strongest
- the most-popular
- the luckiest
- the bravest
- the "coolest"
- the shrewdest

None of these self-delusions is inherently absurd or evil, but each can occupy our attention in ways that distract us from living life's meaning. More than one religion, most notably Zen Buddhism, warns us not to become ensnared by vanities such as these, but apart from advising us to live lives of contemplation, resignation, and compassion, they fail to provide a *reason* for living. Instead, they ask us to adopt a passive state of being, while at the core of human existence is an active wish to give life meaning. The first question is not "How shall we live?," but "Why do we live?"

II

Bliss

The way to find out about your happiness is to keep your mind on those moments when you feel most happy, when you are really happy—not excited, not just thrilled, but deeply happy. This requires a little bit of self-analysis. What is it that makes you happy? Stay with it, no matter what people tell you. This is what I call 'following your bliss.'
—Joseph Campbell, *The Power of Myth*

Imagine that you were invited to make a list of the pleasures that life offers you, the objects and events that make life worthwhile, the experiences or things that make you glad to be alive. If you accept the advice of Joseph Campbell to "follow your bliss," what bliss would you follow? If your life at present is good, what is good about it?

Questions such as these might be summarized as "What is life for?," and the majority response might include events or objects of the following sort:

work	cars	nature
money	movies	gambling
food	travel	hunting
drink	reading	fishing
sleep	gardening	politics
sports	art	ideas
music	pets	numbers

As you cast an eye across this list of life's perquisites, some of them you will endorse as giving meaning to your life, and others will strike you as the odd passions of "people like that." Some of these pursuits will seem entirely too trivial, and the value that people place on them absurd. There may be omissions from the list that the reader finds glaring; those that were omitted purposely include:

1. culture, a concept so ephemeral that no two people agree on what it means; it's so vague that very few people would profess to live for it;

2. health, a necessary ingredient in any pursuit, a kind of minimum requirement for anyone's quest for the good life;

3. worship: some people live to "Praise the Lord" and think of their existence as meaningless unless they are in touch with the Almighty; they seem to believe that the purpose of this life is to have another one; presumably, the second life will not require as much worship as the first.

There are those who love collecting or parades or Bingo or motorcycles or weather or war or fast foods or antiques, etc., but people are not staying alive just to have them or do them, and they would give up their fascination with them to survive. Activities or things such as these were left off the list, because life without them would still be worth living.

The catalogue of life's enjoyments presented above contains a hidden message: with the exception of sports, each object or experience can be a solitary pleasure, i.e., one can savor it and be alone. This exposes the fact that hedonism ("I want to feel good") is essentially narcissistic ("Get out of my way.") in nature. Each person's satisfaction with one of these sources of pleasure is unique to the person and requires no association with another person to be felt as desirable. A person who wants to go fishing does not have to have a companion; making money and spending it can be a solo experience; most gambling involves one person versus "the house," and even in a poker game one's colleagues are antagonists.

Any activity can be shared with someone else, including politics and sleeping, but the pleasure it provides can be separated from the sharing.

This concept of sharing reveals resources for enjoyment of a very different kind, such as:

- love
- sex
- family
- friendship
- camaraderie

What these situations or social systems or states of being have in common is their origin in human relationships. Feeling love, giving love, receiving love—these experiences presuppose the existence of a relationship. real or imagined, consummated or platonic, frivolous or committed. There must be an *other*, as well as a willingness to sacrifice for the other or, at its logical extreme, to lay down one's life for the other. In the words of Camus, "the right to love without limits."

If you can give to a relationship more than you take from it, even more than it asks of you, you will meet every expectation that life has for you. The reason we are on this planet is to establish, maintain, enjoy, and fulfill relationships. In this view, relationship is not everything. It is the only thing.

III

Descartes' Navel

Modern philosophy is formed in the seventeenth century . . . Rene Descartes is the decisive figure in the transition from one era to another. His generation marks the passage from the medieval world to the mature modern spirit.

—Julian Marias, *History of Philosophy*

The French philosopher, Rene Descartes, who wrote in the Seventeenth Century, has been called "the first modern man." The cornerstone of his work is a sentence of three words in Latin that is known to every student of Philosophy 101: *Cogito, ergo sum* (I think, therefore I am.)[1]. The sentiment expressed has the simplicity of an equation, and its publication in *Discourse on Method* in 1637 was then as revolutionary as Einstein's $E=mc^2$. It summarized centuries of attempts to define what "being" means, and served as a preface to centuries of what might be called egocentric logic.

One can imagine the surprise with which Descartes received his revelation, his three-word mantra. Indeed, he struggled to reject the idea but failed, as he tells us in the *Discourse*:

> While I wished to think . . . that everything was false, it necessarily had to be true that I, who was thinking this, was something . . . this truth . . . was so firm and so sure that all the most extravagant suppositions of the skeptic were incapable of shaking it, I judged that I could accept it without a scruple as the first principle of the philosophy I was seeking.[2]

There is no doubt that this proposition is true, but what does it mean? Marias wrote that the *cogito* means: "There

---

[1]   Note the "I" in both clauses.

[2]   As quoted by Marias, J. in *History of Philosophy* (1967) New York: Dover Publications, p. 214.

is nothing certain except myself . . . Philosophy is to be based on 'me' . . . the history of this attempt is the history of modern philosophy."[1] Certainly, Descartes set in motion a chain reaction in Western perceptions of man's identity and place in the universe. For that reason, the unique character of his key insight is worth analyzing.

The *cogito* can be seen as the product of a man given to contemplating his navel in a search for some means to justify his existence. He thinks about something and then thinks about his thinking and on to infinite regress. But, in the process, he decides that the mere act of thinking has value by conferring proof of existence. If he had doubts about who or what he was, he found an effortless way to assuage his fears. He could think about a cabbage and make sure that he occupied some point on the space/time continuum. Moreover, he could assure others that they exist by the sole fact of their thinking of the *cogito* itself or a cabbage, etc., a definite boon to mankind. This conjures up the image of Little Jack Horner:

> Little Jack Horner sat in the corner,
> Eating a Christmas pie.
> He put in his thumb and pulled out a plum,
> And said 'What a good boy am I!'

In effect, Descartes could have said "I see my navel, therefore I am."

---

[1]   Marias, *op. cit.*, p. 215.

A direct intellectual descendant of Descartes was his countryman Jean-Paul Sartre, who wrote: "Man is nothing else but what he makes of himself. Such is the first principle of existentialism."[1] This quintessentially Cartesian theme of "man makes himself," with its isolating, almost paranoid undertones, implies a clear distinction between opposites of these types:

introspection-------interaction
thought-------behavior
self-involvement-------other-directedness
inward-looking-------outward-looking
private-------observable
intuitive-------objective
individualism-------interdependence

The viewpoints on human nature that are listed above on the right-hand side of these dichotomies are explored in this book.

An antithesis to the view that the Self is the center of the universe was offered in *The Meaning of Life*, with these words: *Alter est, ergo sum* (There is another, therefore I am.). The presence of another person is perceived by a sentient observer, who then becomes aware of his or her own existence as a person. The not-me proves me.

---

[1]   Sartre, J.-P., "Existentialism," In Spanos, W. V., *A Casebook on Existentialism*, New York: Thomas Y. Crowell (1966), p. 278.

IV

The Anatomy of Relationship

Psychiatry . . . is the study of processes that involve
or go on between people. The field of psychiatry is
the field of interpersonal relations, under any and
all circumstances in which those relations exist . . .
a personality can never be isolated from the complex
of interpersonal relations in which the person lives
and has his being.

—Harry Stack Sullivan,
Conceptions of Modern Psychiatry

"Relationship," here defined, is the more or less committed, then and now sustained, bond between a person and at least one other person.[1] The relationship originates in at least one interaction between those persons, and it will be modified or closed or extended by interactional events as they occur. One can still have a relationship with someone who is no longer living (loss of interaction), but not with a person whom one has never met (absence of interaction). To understand a relationship, we are obliged to understand the series of interactions that are its building-blocks. The sum of the interactions that a person has experienced with another defines a relationship, and the sum of the relationships that the person has experienced defines a life. How many or how few are a person's relationships is of no importance in this view. The *nature* of each relationship is important, as will be shown in chapters to follow. What you make of your life is not entirely up to you, because each participant in an interaction makes a contribution to the interaction and, by extension, the relationship.

In Psychology, when we study what is happening in, for instance, a two-person interaction, we focus on the *behavior* of one person vis-a-vis the *behavior* of the other. This focal point excludes what either person might be thinking or feeling during the interaction, because those phenomena

---

[1] People and animals have relationships, and of course animals have relationships with other animals, but they are not the subject of this book.

are not directly observable. This approach to understanding why people do what they do is called the *interactional view*. The scientific study of interactions has a long past but a brief history. One twentieth-century milestone was a seminal paper by the anthropologist Gregory Bateson and others, "Toward a Theory of Schizophrenia." First appearing in 1956, this paper reported on the authors' research with the families of schizophrenics. They made word-for-word analyses of audiotapes of communication between family members and the family member who had been labeled "schizophrenic"—in other words, "psychotic" or, in ordinary language, "crazy."[1]

To their surprise, Bateson and his group learned that mixed or self-contradicting statements made by, for

---

[1]   A few words about schizophrenia: this is the worst form of mental illness. It has afflicted people in every part of the world throughout the history of mankind. Its symptoms include hallucinations, delusions, disorganized speech, irrational fears, panic states, poor self-control and, in some instances, self-destructive behavior. In short, this is what we mean by "madness," and not too many years ago people were locked-up for much of their lives because of it. Some say that there is no cure for schizophrenia, while others believe that the symptoms can at least be alleviated by certain drugs, even if a complete cure cannot be guaranteed; this belief is based on the theory that schizophrenia is a "brain disease" that can be treated by altering brain chemistry. Still others believe that schizophrenia is genetically transmitted which, if true, is disheartening because the alteration of human genetic structure is not yet possible.

example, a parent to a child, could affect the child so profoundly that he or she would develop odd forms of behavior or odd patterns of language. In extreme cases, such as those of people who eventually require psychiatric hospitalization, it was shown that these causal forces could have lifelong effects that are essentially irreversible.

The mechanism by which this process works can be described by a simple example: a young boy makes a critical comment to his mother. She says "You didn't mean to say that." The boy says "Yes, I did," and the mother replies "No, you didn't. I only tell you this because I love you." The boy, in order to accept the mother's protestation of love, must retract his critical comment; therefore, he must not criticize in order to be loved. In their analysis of a similar situation, Bateson, *et al.*, wrote:

> " . . . the easiest path for the child is to accept the mother's simulated loving behavior as real, and his desires to interpret what is going on are undermined. Yet the result is that the mother is withdrawing from him and defining this withdrawal as the way a loving relationship should be." (*op. cit.*, p. 42)

In another example, contradictory messages are sent by one person in an interaction to the other by nonverbal means, as when a mother says to a child "Let me give you a hug," and then retreats as the child moves forward with arms outstretched or, conversely, hugs the child so tightly as to threaten breathing, while saying something like "I love you to death."

The most widely-known fictional description of mixed messages such as these occurs in Joseph Heller's *Catch-22*. Yossarian, an Air Force bombardier in World War II, develops a suffocating fear of continuing the bombing missions to which he has been assigned. He tells his commanding officer that he cannot fly again because he has become mentally ill. The commanding officer reminds him that anyone who goes on missions as dangerous as these would have to be crazy to do so. But, since Yossarian does not want to go, he must be sane; therefore, he must fly more missions. That is Catch-22.

Bateson and his colleagues used a different term: they called this psychological beartrap "the double bind." It is "double" because the person who is caught in it (1) cannot resolve its contradiction and (2) cannot escape the trap that the relationship demands. This is truly a no-win situation: one is damned if one does and damned if one doesn't. The result literally boggles the mind. This state, when repeated or prolonged, is the starting-point for the disordered perceptions and bizarre behaviors of schizophrenia—according to the theory presented here. There is, in this view, no contributing hereditary factor, because these causal forces originate in the person's environment. And even if the proximate cause of schizophrenia is abnormal brain chemistry, the question remains: what caused the brain chemistry to be abnormal in the first place? The ultimate cause of schizophrenia must be something that *happens to* the person. How does it happen? Someone makes it happen. How is it done?: by word or gesture, by a tone of voice or the look of a face. The origin of severe mental illness is the same as the origin of most human misery: the way people treat each-other.

Schizophrenia is not a subject of this book. The topic is introduced here to illustrate the power of human interaction. People control people. The behavior of person A determines the behavior of person B, and vice versa. And this principle can be applied to behavior in its simplest form as well as the most complex—insanity.

The largely unknown prophet of this interactional view was the psychiatrist Harry Stack Sullivan. In 1939, Sullivan was invited to give the first series of William Alanson White Foundation lectures in Washington, D.C.; the lectures were subsequently published in the journal *Psychiatry,* and later in book form as *Conceptions of Modern Psychiatry* (New York: W.W. Norton, 1940). They began a revolution in psychological thinking that has remained subconscious for decades, but has influenced many innovations in theory and practice. By defining "a personality" as a "complex of interpersonal relations," he gave a new perspective not only to the study of disorders of personality but to normal mental functioning as well. Patrick Mullahy, in his chapter in the same book, clarifies this paradigm shift in the way we attempt to understand human behavior, as follows:

. . . one discovers that it is not a person *as an isolated and self-contained entity* that one is studying . . . but a situation, an interpersonal situation, composed of two or more people.[1]

(In the service of brevity, the terms "interpersonal relations" and "interpersonal situation" can be represented by "interaction(s)" as used in this book.)

Naturally, Sullivan's viewpoint and the definitional concepts that he derived from it were not well received by the psychiatric community, then dominated intellectually by the psychoanalysts. Freud's therapy was inward-looking, intended to find the sources of a person's problems in the deepest recesses of the psyche; the concept of the unconscious (or subconscious) mind was not a purely Freudian invention, but probing it became the guiding principle of his methods of therapy. Imagine how antithetical was the idea that the sources of a person's problems are not internal but external to the person. Moreover, they are to be found in the behavior of *another* person.

Far beyond the theory and practice of psychotherapy, this interpretation of the causes of behavior has much to say about human nature. If we see people as interdependent in what they do, we may start from the same perspective when we think about *who they are*. According to this perspective, people are:

---

[1]   Mullahy, P. "A Theory of Interpersonal Relations and the Evolution of Personality." In Sullivan, H.S., (1940), *op. cit.*, p. 245.

- environmentally determined
- guided by others
- guiding toward others
- constantly interacting
- enmeshed in relationships

These descriptors of the human condition imply that men and women are not pawns of Fate or servants of God; they are not genetically-programmed, and anatomy is not their destiny. No amount of "breeding," luck-of-the-gods, or force of will can produce the *ubermensch* of Nietzsche and Hitler. Nor do people conform to the beliefs of that rugged individualist, Ayn Rand, who wrote:

> Civilization is the progress toward a society of privacy. The savage's whole existence is public, ruled by the laws of his tribe. Civilization is the process of setting man free from men.[1]

If we take the interactional view to its logical extension, it stands in direct opposition to the notions of Free Will and self-determination. If what a person wills occurs in the context of a relationship, then it expresses more than one person's will. One cannot act alone because one is not alone.

Exposing the Myth of Individuality is a cornerstone of this approach to understanding people. The Cult of the Self

---

[1]   Rand, A. *The Fountainhead* (1943), New York: the Bobbs-Merrill Company, p.p. 684-685.

is not simply immoral, it relies on a defective psychology. A person is not a self-governing entity. Human acts do not emerge from within, originating in a self-contained behavioral engine. People do what they do in reaction to what others do to them. In turn, what a person does influences what the other does as well, in a circle of cause and effect, effect and cause. To say that we are self-willed is to omit half of the equation, and thus to arrive at a mistaken answer.

By way of examples of this process at work, we know that people are taught bigotry; they are taught to take what belongs to others and to be violent and the arts of war and every other antisocial act. These are not the products of malnutrition or a hormone imbalance or a defective gene or a diseased brain or demonic possession. People learn because they are taught by teachers who, whether by means of demonstration or command, give them lessons. A final irony is that the one who teaches may not even be aware of giving the lesson, thus evading the consequences of guilt. This phenomenon, of course, is only a result of the most corrupt form of interaction, occurring in the most pathological kind of relationship. In sum, even though relationship is the only thing, it is not always a good thing.

Where is the proof of these assertions? Partial proof was offered in describing the etiology of schizophrenia. To review, this terrible illness is created, induced, inflicted on unsuspecting victims by people who are entrusted with their care. Further proof will be offered in the next chapter, in which an even more horrific product of the force of relationship will be analyzed.

V

Proof of the Thesis

I do not need to tell you . . . how hatefully conceived
and executed many suicides really are . . . if you
know a family situation in which such an event has
occurred you will be impressed with the fact that
the self-destruction had an evil effect, and may well
have been calculated to have a prolonged evil effect
on some other people . . . a hateful combination of
impulses which leads to destroying oneself in order
to strike at some other person.

—Harry Stack Sullivan,
Conceptions of Modern Psychiatry

There are many causes for a suicide, and generally the
most obvious ones were not the most powerful . . .
Newspapers often speak of 'personal sorrows' or of

'incurable illness.' These explanations are plausible. But one would have to know whether a friend of the desperate man had not that very day addressed him indifferently. He is the guilty one.

—Albert Camus, *The Myth of Sisyphus*

In this chapter, I shall describe the stark reality of relationship gone wrong. Here I present relationship in its ugliest form—as an agent of death. Only in this way can we appreciate its transcendent power to create the Good Life.

Before taking up the task of describing the Worst Relationship, I can place the subject in a general context: it concerns the nature of human feelings. I made a list of the basic emotions that people feel, and after listing fifty or so—from admiration to lust, from jealousy to rage, pride to shame—I saw that most of them fit roughly into two major categories that could be distinguished as positive or negative, hurtful or helpful, life-affirming or life-denying. As labels differentiating these two types of emotion, many pairs of opposite terms might come to mind, but my preference is for these: love and anger.

If you think of love as a force that draws people together, by contrast with anger as a force that pushes people apart, or if you use the analogy of magnetic attraction and repulsion, you will see that these two classes of emotion are as diametrically opposed as good and evil. And, as with good and evil, their qualities are mutually exclusive: they might occur alternately, but one cannot be loving and angry at the same time.

The usefulness of this love-anger dichotomy can be shown by applying it to an understanding of the motives for human behavior ("Motive" and "emotion" are words derived from the same root.) When we look for the "driving force" behind an action, we can expect to find it in one or more of the core feelings that are listed in Table 1, which are classified according to their affinities to the passions of love or anger.

Table 1[1]

HUMAN FEELINGS

POSITIVE	NEGATIVE
joy	fear
happiness	sadness
elation	rage
lust	terror
excitement	hostility
attraction	loneliness
passion	anger
love	tension

---

[1] This list is not meant to be exhaustive. Most readers will be aware of other true feelings that might be added. The list is merely intended to illustrate the dichotomy between love and anger. There are feelings that, taken in context, could belong in either category, e.g., pity, surprise, longing, curiosity, astonishment.

affection   shame

sympathy   embarrassment

empathy   shyness

ebullience   envy

euphoria   jealousy

admiration   loathing

awe   contempt

relief   disdain

calmness   despair

compassion   sorrow

esteem   grief

arousal   despondency

confidence   indifference

courage   hatred

desire   boredom

trust   "numbness"

                     disgust

                     horror

                     suspicion

Feelings are neither right nor wrong, good nor evil; they are natural attributes of animal existence. Of course, the actions that they motivate can be evil, but the fault lies with the act not the emotion. Hatred, for example, is not a crime, while assault and murder are crimes. In sum, love and anger are the two great emotional forces that fuel the engine of life. A logical extension of this view is that, when we try to find out why people behave in some way, often asking "What made him do that?," we can begin the inquiry by asking whether the act was motivated by love or anger. This logical framework might indeed be used to explain extreme human behaviors such as rape or murder or, as in the following pages, suicide.

Much of what is known about suicide comes from (a) successful efforts at prevention, (b) inferences drawn from suicide notes, or (c) because notes are rarely left, what we can learn from post-hoc interviews with relatives and friends who are the victims of completed suicides—a process called the "psychological autopsy." Quite apart from the fact that this is one subject that cannot be studied experimentally—because of the lethal risk to the object of study—the entire topic is obscured by taboo and superstition.

Why are we afraid of confronting this one among the many social ills? No one but the most sociopathic religious fanatic would *advocate* suicide. Everyone who learns about a death like this is perplexed and troubled by it. Surely, any suicide is a tragedy, and any increase in the suicide rate would be an indictment of the culture in which it occurs. The fact that approximately 30,000 people kill themselves in the United States each year is deplored by bureaucrats and sociologists alike; it is even, by many in the "helping professions," acknowledged as a mark of failure. In one telling example, clinical psychology, through its official journal, recently declared that there are no proven methods of preventing suicide and no accepted direction for research on the causes of suicidal behavior.[1] This grim confession by the professionals would be less daunting if everyone else would apply common sense to the problem, but there is a powerful stigma that stifles curiosity about self-murder. We prefer not to think about it and, as a result, would rather not study it—as though, if we disturbed the tomb, a curse would fall upon us. As a topic of discussion, it is as distasteful as incest; so, having declared our outrage at both, we try to put them out of mind. In fact, the more powerful is the taboo against some human act, the more resistant it is to understanding, because emotion clouds our powers of reasoning.

So, we turn our backs on the social ill of suicide, and try to ignore it. But some of us cannot do that, because we have known someone who has committed suicide, and the issue forces itself upon us. When I speak on this subject at seminars, I begin by telling the audience that I am aware that someone in attendance may have lost a family member or loved-one to suicide. I apologize in advance if my message seems harsh or unfeeling. There is seldom any immediate response from the audience, but invariably, at the end of the session, at least one person will come forward to say that his or her life has been touched by a suicidal death.

The message that I have to offer is inevitably harsh, calling attention as it does to the baser human instincts.

[1] Rudd, M.D. and Joiner, T. (1998) *Clinical Psychology: Science and Practice*, v. 5, n 2, Summer, pp. 135-150.

The suicidal impulse arises from the darkest part of human character. No one has made this point more eloquently than the French essayist, Albert Camus, who wrote, about suicide, "An act like this is prepared within the silence of the heart, as is a great work of art."[1] He meant that this act is:

1. the product of conscious decision, i.e., chosen;
2. calculated, planned; the plan is:
3. veiled, kept secret, hidden from others until revealed by the act's completion.

The reason for such stealth is obvious when one considers the savagery of what is being "prepared."

Suicide, the one evil action for which its perpetrator cannot be held accountable, is a cold-blooded attack by a person on another person. Its purpose is to punish the person who lives, by and on behalf of the person who dies. In short, a suicidal act occurs in the context of a relationship that has gone horribly wrong. The death of one partner in the relationship is intended to "mark," with an indelible brand, the one who lives on and must accept perpetual guilt. In this way, self-murder is transformed into "murder"—committed by the survivor who will be blamed for the death. That target of blame becomes, in the eyes of others, a "murderer" who will be held responsible *ad infinitum*. Thus suicide is born of a hatred that roils and festers in the heart. This hatred is not, contrary to conventional wisdom, a hatred of the self, but hatred of another, for which suicide is the only available expression.

From the grave, the suicide's voice cries out, with the cold fury of revenge: "GAME OVER: I won. Your life will never be the same. Every day, you will remember what I did and be sorry for what you have done to me. Other people will remind you if you forget; they will act as agents in my torture of you. You cannot escape their scorn." This is how one person in a relationship has chosen to change the terms of the relationship, which has come to an end only in a technical sense. These two people are joined, in soul and spirit, as long as one of them lives.

A poignant example of the way in which the dead and the living dance on is that of the poet Ted Hughes and his poetess wife, Sylvia Plath, whose spiritual bond grew *stronger* after her suicidal death.[1] Even so, it is not necessary to look, for lessons, to the well-publicized suicides of famous people. Indeed, the possibility of this kind of denouement exists in every human relationship. But only in the most intimate and intense liaison can such vindictive hatred occur, and the fact that it seldom occurs tells us everything about the healing grace of love. If relationship gone wrong can destroy life, relationship fulfilled gives it meaning.

---

[1] This tragic relationship that culminated in suicide is analyzed in detail in Everstine, L. *The Anatomy of Suicide: Silence of the Heart* (1998) Springfield, Illinois: Charles C. Thomas, pp. 62-70.

In summary, death by suicide:

1. is a willed action;
2. assures that at least one other person will be punished by it;
3. intends to enact revenge.

This means that suicide, the renunciation of life, is an act of spite. It is relationship-bound and relationship-driven. A person aims his or her death like a weapon, at or toward another person, the target, who must bear responsibility for it. If destruction of life is a conscious choice to end a relationship, staying alive is an affirmation of the value of a relationship.

Just as some people kill themselves to end a malignant relationship, the vast majority reject suicide by affirming a valued relationship. As a Psychologist, I have observed the truth of this assertion in a real-life context, namely that of a mother who has threatened suicide; no single deterrent to a suicidal death is more powerful than this simple question: "What about your children?" Every woman knows that being a mother demands selflessness, and most mothers know that there is nothing selfless about suicide. Living because of others signifies more than just courage: it imbues one with the spirit of the Life Force itself. We live in, by, and for relationships, and they are too precious to waste. Mothers understand this better than do other life forms.

VI

The Evolution of Relationship

... when I met you, suddenly I was no longer afraid ... It still seems incredible to me that I managed to get both—the 'love of my life' and the identity with my own person. And yet I achieved the one only since I also have the other. But finally I ... know what happiness is.

> —letter from Hannah Arendt to
> Heinrich Blucher, her husband

The mind has a thousand eyes,
And the heart but one;
Yet the light of a whole life dies
When love is done.

> —"The Night Has a Thousand Eyes,"
> Francis William Bourdillon

What is the role of relationship in the Cosmic Plan? What connection does it have with the evolution of species? what is its significance for the rise of civilization, or conversely its decline and fall? If relationship is a cornerstone, what is built upon it? If it is a capstone, what bears its weight? If the meaning of life is relationship, what is the meaning of relationship? What are its properties and dimensions, its limits and its potentiality? How can we get the most out of our relationships and, by extension, our lives? From the Alpha of a mother's bond with her newborn child, to the Omega of a suicide who severs a bond by destroying himself, what is the landscape of that valley between?

When I wrote that the meaning of life is relationship, I was not referring to "relationship" in any metaphorical sense, nor was I proposing it as an abstract principle. People form and cultivate (and aggravate) relationships of gaze and touch and breath and sweat, by terms of endearment and wounding curses. Their relations with other people have a palpable reality that is no less real for being hard to appraise or value. The bonds that connect people are neither mystical nor symbolic. The connection is not a Oneness of Being or a collective unconscious or a Brotherhood of Man or any other fantasy of relatedness. Flesh-and-blood people love each-other or kill each-other (among other sorrows) for flesh-and-blood reasons. Sex, to be sure, is part of the equation, but because it has as much power to damage a bond as to strengthen it, the significance of sex to a relationship must be kept in perspective. As will be shown later in this book, sex is not the purpose of relationship, nor is relationship a goal of sex. Sex without relationship is best understood as a form of rape, and relationship without sex is a common phenomenon.

Stripped of illusion and wishful thinking, relationship can be observed, analyzed, and understood objectively and dispassionately, as a process that has its characteristic ebbs and flows and stages of development. A relationship evolves as follows.[1]

AWARENESS

Great poems and songs have been written about moments of truth such as meeting someone for the first time and feeling shocked or confused or thunderstruck or otherwise bedazzled. Relationships do not all start this way, but this form of revelation tells us that a romantic relationship is definitely possible. The word "chemistry" has no connotation that can convey this experience adequately, since the experience is *recognition* at its most primitive source. For example, it could be recognition of the contours of a mother's or a father's face, or the face of a lost love, in the new face being observed. There is magic and mystery in this first perception of the other, and these sensations may never be understood by the observer, because they occur at a subconscious level. When we say "Beauty is in the eye of the beholder," we

---

[1] The process described here uses the romantic or love relationship as a prototype of the many varieties of relationship.

accept that the beholder may have no idea of why it looks that way to him.

ATTRACTION

Each of us, by the time of young adulthood, has constructed a mental model of the ideal face and form of a potential mate. Of course, none of this programming is "known" to us, but, in the subconscious mind, our selection process is governed by our needs and those needs are primordial. Again, "chemistry" is misleading, because it is too weak to describe what is happening, which is more like the shift in tectonic plates that precedes an earthquake; it is much more than the product of hormonal secretion. This process of attraction begins in a way of thinking about what one is seeing, and the hormones follow suit—just as sexual feelings are preceded by sexual thoughts.

COMMUNICATION

There is a desperate need, on the part of each of the newly-discovered partners, to know what this compelling attraction means. Rather than ask directly, a false step that could break the "spell," each person conducts a fact-finding mission to find out "who she is" or "where is he coming from?" This involves a lot of idle chatter, only rarely believable, in which the two relate various versions of their life histories, just partially true, to impress and reassure. They may even make mention of some of their aspirations for the future, each one carefully floating it by the other to see what response it gets, as for example: "My parents will be leaving me the farm" or "I've always wanted to travel." This is the kind of repartee that Noel Coward satirized so well—totally vacuous, but absolutely essential to helping an early interaction off the ground.

DESIRE

This and the next development, Understanding, are often juxtaposed, depending on the unfulfilled needs of the participants at the time. Two people have met, each has been mutually attracted to the other, they have tried to find a shared channel of communication, and now the natural processes of lust and curiosity demand attention. Physical desire is the more heated when its object is an enigma, a mystery to be solved. Who has never asked the question "I wonder what he (she) is like in bed"? Sooner or later, the question must be answered, but it is foolish to believe that the answer is sought more urgently in the Twenty-first Century than it was in Roman times. Here, we are dealing with primitive impulses, as involuntary as the urge to survive or the need to worship a "higher power," or the wish to live forever. Not many adult relationships can ignore this exploration or delay it indefinitely.

UNDERSTANDING

Whether or not lust has been satisfied, the development of a relationship requires a period of curious contemplation of each person by the other. This process is markedly different from those of "making acquaintance" or "becoming friends" or even "knowing" in the Biblical sense. It is now necessary to figure out what makes the partner "tick," and this happens far more subtly and in much more depth than the superficial fact-finding that typifies the infatuation phase. Now, for example, occurs the requisite quarrel, reaffirming the adage that no friendship is formed until after two people have had their first fight. Sometimes, feelings are so damaged that the lovers must separate for a time to re-assess the relationship. Often, this time apart is beneficial to the bond that is forming, because each feels "lost" without the other.

If and when the two recover from their earliest misunderstanding, they can get on with the "business" of this stage in the relationship, in which each tries to discover what the other wants out of life. Already, a person knows a lot about the other's *preferences*. e.g., cold weather over warm, privacy over sociability, a tranquil life versus a life of excitement, steak versus chicken. But, now is the time to learn about what he or she *values*, as for instance work (versus pleasure), action (versus contemplation), faith (versus certainty), spending what you have (versus saving for a rainy day), family or group (versus individual or self).

Our values are signposts that guide the way we live and templates on which we build belief-systems. They tell us what is important, what is worth doing, and they help us select between equal-appearing alternatives. Psychologists believe that values are deeply ingrained within us by the age of nine. For the most part, we are not totally aware of these beliefs, and tend to keep them secret from others as well as ourselves. This reticence is natural early on, when taking too firm a stand on one value-laden choice against another might derail courtship, but "little white lies" at this stage can cause trouble down the road. For instance, many marriage counselors have worked with couples who, let us say, were courting for five years and married for ten, only to hear one spouse tell the other something like "I had no idea that the Church meant so much to you." But, when partners disclose to each-other as much as they understand about their own affinities and prejudices, they can move toward the next stage in the evolution of their relationship: acceptance.

ACCEPTANCE

To know someone is not necessarily to love that person. This truism is the theme of a vital stage in the development of a relationship, in which reality begins to assert its domination over wishful thinking. Here begins to form, as well, the saving grace of forgiveness that will serve the relationship well in years to come. One partner gradually recognizes that the other's values and preferences are well ingrained and not likely to be changed in large measure. Some habits are not likely to be broken; these must be acknowledged and accepted as fixed attributes, as natural and as innocent as the shape of the other's nose. "She doesn't get along with my family, but she's still a good person"; "I hate war, but I know that he is proud of being a veteran"; "I guess she hasn't forgiven me for suggesting an abortion."

Eventually, these differences of opinion and belief and loyalty and style are assimilated into a relationship in the way that light through a prism emerges as a single beam. At this crossroad, many a relationship is lost for lack of acceptance of the other's "faults." What happens is that the frequency and volume of bickering over trivia becomes unbearable to one or both; the trivial matters themselves are merely surface details that stand for hidden fissures in the couple's system of values. If they don't agree, for example, about the importance of money or the part that money matters should play in a person's life, they may quarrel, with time, about even the most trifling purchase. If this mutual lack of acceptance continues, it may lead to one of those power struggles that even the most committed partners experience occasionally. This is the equivalent of what happens when each of two dancers tries to "lead" in the dance simultaneously.

The only antidote to a power struggle is compromise on the part of both antagonists. This can take the form of permitting power to alternate between two people by taking turns; or, power can be divided between the two people by subject: one makes travel arrangements and the other is in charge of entertainment and dinners out; one pays the bills and the other keeps up social correspondence. This does not require *agreement* on how a task should be done. It relies on *acceptance* of the other's capacity for doing it.

ADMIRATION

With time together in the relationship, and given that acceptance of the other has been achieved, two people can begin to savor their relationship for itself. Relationship has taken on a life of its own and, in the security it provides, each can begin to see the other clearly, critically, and ultimately admiringly. In the ideal case, correctional factors will have been applied to the other's "faults," and power struggles resolved through compromise. This will enable each to see the other's virtues and appreciate them. Friends and family will describe it as a "stable" relationship, and the partners can indulge themselves on occasion by remarking on their good fortune in having met.

INTERDEPENDENCE

It's said that two who form a couple become more alike with the passing years, but that saying may be a result of their friends' biased perception of the union. A more incisive observation might be that the partners display their *need* for each-other; i.e., their complementarity "shows." And whether it shows or not, this complementarity is felt by the partners whenever they pause to reflect on the relationship instead of just living it. This growing need is reminiscent of the time when the two had just met and were lost in the fog of Attraction, when every moment out of the sight of the other was exquisite agony.

When they are interdependent, two people need each-other in the best way: when the other is not present, a wistful longing appears, as though one part of the self were missing. We feel this way because we have incorporated some of the traits and attributes of the other person into ourselves, and we need to replenish the ego with these traits to remain whole. Loneliness is what we feel when the most valuable elements of ourselves have gone or are beyond reach, and our sadness comes from being left with the defective half. Each feels the other's absence like an angry wound. When the sound of the door being opened announces the other's return, a sense of freedom is felt, because one can return to being an intact self. What a paradox it is that, when two people are closer than ever, the uniqueness of each can be more freely expressed. In this way, interdependence fosters individuality.

The importance of becoming one's true self through an interdependent relationship lies in being prepared for the intimation of mortality that both will experience, sooner than later. One person's need for the other will assert itself in ways that neither could have imagined, and their needs will seldom be equal. "Being there" for the other person might have been an empty phrase until now, but with interdependence it doesn't have to be forced; it is part of a natural process.

NEED

When someone is "there" for you, and willingly, the depredations of aging and the narrowing of one's horizons will be easier to bear. The relationship is fortunate in which both partners feel their powers waning at about the same time, but one must be ready to accept that a partner's timetable may differ from one's own.

There is no sense in dwelling on this maudlin topic, but the fact is that relationship may culminate in a desperate need for the other person's help, or in the other person's desperate need for help. The odds are overwhelming that one partner will die well before the other does, and this prelude to death may be just as one-sided.

In their halcyon days, members of a couple often say to themselves "I'm so happy that we can grow old together." It's a lovely sentiment, but I think of what a friend, then in his seventies, told me once: "Don't get old—you won't like it." Those who must face this reality are blessed if they have a lasting relationship and do not have to face that reality alone.

LOSS

Fate exacts a terrible price for relationship, because it invariably takes away one partner before the other. Naturally, the more devoted the relationship, the more catastrophic the loss; the stronger the bond, the more likely the survivor will have been diminished by half. Half a person can live, but only on memories. Happiness becomes Before and After, Then and Now, the inevitable comparison and contrast with "when she was alive." The Life Force sees our suffering and regards it with cold logic: we should have known what we were getting into.

What we were getting into is a chance for the only afterlife we shall ever achieve, the life we live in the minds and hearts of the ones we left behind. Some people want to leave a "legacy," some a fortune, but the most they can leave is a feeling of loss in those who cared about them when alive.[1]

Relationship never dies. It lives on by being more than the sum of the partners, in the "we" of "we did" and "we had" and "we went" and "we felt" and "we saw" and "we thought" and "we decided" and "we planned" and "we settled for" and "we couldn't quite" and "if only we." The "we" of expectation, of yearning, of a story never ending will outlive both partners, and will never be copied by any two others. What the relationship left undone is the closest either comes to immortality.

REMEMBRANCE

The trouble with grief is its self-referential nature. We have a tendency to focus on our feelings of loss, instead of the lost person. That, too, will pass, but until it does our remembrance of the relationship can be clouded by self-pity. Eventually, our appreciation for the lost partner will return, borne on our memories of the good times. In the words of a song:

> Mem'ry.
> All alone in the moonlight

---

[1] The suicide, of course, leaves other emotions. These observations apply only to involuntary death.

> I can smile at the old days,
> I was beautiful then. I remember the time
> I knew what happiness was,
> Let the mem'ry live again.[1]

Now that remembrance is all that we have of relationship, a person needs to know how best to cherish a memory. We practice this, from time to time when the other is away for some reason, and we comfort ourselves by conjuring up the other's face in the mind's eye, or recalling some event when the relationship was most harmonious. The exercise is bittersweet, because the vividness of the memory reminds us of how little we appreciated the warmth it gave us when it happened. This is the point made by "Our Town," Thornton Wilder's classic play, in which a character says:

> It goes so fast. We don't have time to look at one another . . . O, earth, you're too wonderful for anybody to realize you . . . Do any human beings ever realize life while they live it?—every, every minute?[2]

And if we didn't fully understand what it meant to us at the time, now we can recall and revere it as a souvenir. The partner who has lost someone can find the best part in

---

[1]   Nunn, T. "Memory," from "Cats."

[2]   Wilder, T. *Our Town* (1957), New York: Harper & Row, p. 100.

every memory of their relationship, and embellish it with feelings that were never present at the time; for example, a memory of the day they first met, with all its excitement and wonder, might be remembered with tears of joy.

VII

Seven Lively Sins

"Oh, Carrie, Carrie! Oh, blind strivings of the human heart! . . . In your rocking-chair, by your window dreaming, shall you long, alone. In your rocking-chair, by your window, shall you dream such happiness as you may never feel."
—Theodore Dreiser: last lines of *Sister Carrie*

The Sixth Century Pope, St. Gregory the Great, gave us the Seven Deadly Sins, namely Pride, Envy, Wrath, Lust, Gluttony, Avarice, and Sloth. These are "deadly" only in metaphor, of course, and do not even warrant damnation in Hell. In fact, Dante made them into terraces on the mountain of Purgatory; the penitent climbs from level to level, expiating one sin after another, on the journey to Paradise.

In a secular world, sin is its own punishment. If we have only one life, there are no suspended sentences and no otherworldly repentance. The penalty is enforced here-and-now, and each sin we commit must be corrected within a lifetime. If not absolved, we live out our time in misery. The bus to Purgatory stops here.

You may have noticed that the sins of today are not those of Sixth Century Christianity. This is not because people are different, but because our values differ. The peccadilloes that St. Gregory believed were offensive to God are with us still, but we see them in another light. To be sure, the faults of envy and avarice are commonplace and deplorable, but lust and wrath are basic functions of the human condition; we accept them as immutable, and make rules to confine them within reasonable limits. So, too, with gluttony and sloth; we recognize them as weaknesses, but the harm they do is mostly to the self. Pride, by contrast, can be a positive emotion, especially if there is no further need to be humble in the face of a god.[1]

---

[1]   Conceit is the corruption of pride, and may be the fault that St. Gregory had in mind.

The sins of everyday life, as we live it now, are "lively" because they lurk in every person and are taken for granted as "human nature." Nevertheless, they are no less harmful for being familiar. We avoid acknowledging these "lesser" versions of sin and content ourselves, in our minds, with remaining innocent of the canonical versions.

These all-too-human traits and temptations are six of the Seven Lively Sins:

- indifference
- deceit
- work
- jealousy
- fantasy
- waste

They are more than weaknesses or bad habits or idle passions or mere defects of character; instead, they are crimes of the heart because they threaten to destroy relationships. In doing so, they devalue life.

How are relationships weakened, endangered, broken? We have seen, in Chapter V, that a wrecked relationship can be lethal to one or both of the partners. Relationships decay from within, through a series of interactions in which one partner, in essence, fails the other. In that respect, relationships are as frail as the body itself. Among the main causes of infection are the viruses described below.

WORK

This artifact of human existence is seldom thought-of as "sinful," but because we take it for granted as a condition of life, its meaning is rarely examined. Of course, people work to live, but this examination concerns work for work's sake, as though working itself were a virtue. The sinful part is living to work.

Parkinson's Law holds that "Work expands to fill the time available for its completion." If this is true, it happens because people permit it to happen, and it may be that they want it to be so. Why do people take up their burdens so willingly? The most common cause is thought to be the "Protestant work ethic"—often blamed on Calvin or Luther, even though many religions and cultures share its precepts. The idea that hard work is an intrinsic good is embellished by the notion that Earthly diligence is proof of piety and will be rewarded later on. If that is the case, available work is a blessing.

Relationships, for better or worse, are Earthbound creatures that require nourishment and care. Freud's *lieben und arbeiten* (love and work) identifies the two hemispheres at the core of one's existence. In the modern world, most people alternate between these hemispheres, with cyclical variations, for the better part of adult life. Normally, the two reciprocate harmoniously, as when the wounds of the boiler room are cleansed in the bedroom, and a tribulation at the breakfast table is calmed at the conference table. It is when one partner, usually male, forms an obsession with his work that the trouble begins. The workaholic husband and father trades his loved-ones for his colleagues on the job.

Work is a transgression against relationship when it takes time and energy away from the interactions that are the life blood of the central relationships of our lives. The cause is the profound egotism of one partner, in which he steals their lives from those closest to him. Bernard Shaw wrote: "Nothing makes a man so selfish as work." For such a man, it is "my job," "my mission," "my calling," "my task" (e.g., MEIN KAMPF). The job is his place in the universe and his possession. The man who is "married to his work" is married to no one.

Everyone knows a couple driven apart by one person's addiction to work. Juvenile Halls are crowded with kids whose fathers neglected them or whose mothers felt a need to give the family a second income. Work itself is impassionate, sweeping aside everything in its path. After 40 years, it spits out the wage slave, leaving him or her to wonder what happened. "Where did my life go?" It was consumed in the maw of the work ethic.

Even in well-recognized and highly-regarded work there is no ultimate consolation. The person who finds a cure for cancer has not conquered death by other means, nor death itself by any means. This reminds us how transient and inconsequential are the works of Man. Man's accomplishments are never sufficient to the need thereof.

JEALOUSY

Unlike envy, which is wanting what someone else has, jealousy is wanting someone not to have what you could have. The motive for jealousy begins with possession, real or imagined, and ends in possessiveness—a primitive, animalistic trait. There is no more dangerous emotion than jealousy, and the behavior it inspires is barbaric. Its core dynamics are paranoid, but the root cause lies at a deeper level, in the person's pervasive and suffocating sense of inferiority.

The feeling of inferiority is like a cancerous growth that can spread its venom throughout the personality. It is extremely resistant to treatment by therapeutic means; in effect, one cannot be talked into self-confidence. The only remedy for a person who lacks self-esteem is for him or her to have a series of positive experiences, interspersed with as few negative experiences as possible. In short, success drives out the fear of failure.

Naturally, few people are lucky enough to enjoy a series of signal victories in their lives, and many others are left with self-doubt and fragile egos. This kind of person, when invested in a relationship, is easy prey for Shakespeare's "green-ey'd monster." Jealousy lowers the threshold for suspicion, and any action of the loved-one can be taken as proof of betrayal. "The ear of jealousy heareth all things," we are told,[1] and in this state of heightened awareness the jealous partner questions

---

[1] *The Wisdom of Solomon*, 1:10.

every word. The loved-one, in turn, is offended by not being trusted and burns with resentment. If the jealous accusations continue, the relationship will grow cold, in some cases becoming abusive. Only the jealous person can stop this process, as with any bad habit, by force of will.

Jealousy is a devilish emotion that serves no useful purpose in human life. From *The Song of Solomon* we learn that "jealousy is cruel as the grave."[1] Shakespeare taught the same lesson: both Desdemona and Othello are dead before the final curtain.

DECEIT

It is said that Italian men have perfected the art of adultery; presumably, their secret formula consists in denying, eternally, that they are having an affair. According to custom, the wives are to have their suspicions but not ask too many questions. As shown in many movies, what happens when they find out is explosive but not necessarily tragic.

In other societies, where games like this are not as common, infidelity can devastate a relationship because it falsifies the stated or implied relationship contract. Even so, for every relationship that is wrecked by infidelity, another is rebuilt by means of apology and forgiveness.

The lively sin of deceit has many more subtle variations than infidelity, and these are much less often resolved.

---

[1] *The Song of Solomon,* 7:10.

They are the lies that people tell each-other and by which they harm a relationship in a misguided attempt to help it. We normally refer to these as "white" lies, which are white until they are found out. Then there are lies that are intended to conceal the fact of a previous lie. Sir Walter Scott wrote "Oh what a tangled web we weave, when first we practice to deceive," because lies beget lies. And even when we are not being false on purpose to manipulate or cover up, we can lie without saying a word by withholding the truth. This is especially true in dysfunctional families, in which secrets are kept by some members and not revealed to others. Because it omits telling the truth, the secret is a tacit lie; an example would be when several members of a family dislike a new in-law, but keep quiet about it to "protect" the spouse.

Here are other examples of deceit *in vivo*:

- A man tells his wife that she is the most beautiful woman in the world and then turns to look at every woman who passes by.
- A woman flirts with her boss until she gets her promotion.
- An adolescent tells his mother he is going to the library, and then goes to the mall.
- A bride waits until after the wedding to tell the groom that she is pregnant.
- A young man pays court to an elderly woman until he is mentioned in her will.

When the deception is revealed, there follows blame and, in turn, guilt; in this way, both deceiver and deceived feel wronged. Many a relationship eventually erodes under pressures such as these. Some people are capable of forgiving the act being lied about, but cannot condone the cover-up. Others can tolerate deceit as a natural attempt to avoid discovery, while they condemn the act itself. In either case, the relationship suffers an indelible wound.

FANTASY

Fantasy consists in thinking of things that never happened. They could have but didn't. They might but not yet. Children dwell in this mode of thinking much of the time, inventing a reality for themselves in the process: the little girl becomes the mother of her dolls, and the little boy becomes his action figure. In dreams, our subconscious mind gives us narrative, plot, and characters, and in daydreams the conscious mind takes us wherever we want to go. Shakespeare understood how trivial and misleading are these excursions into the void:

> I talk of dreams
> Which are the children of an idle brain,
> Begot of nothing but vain fantasy.[1]

---

[1]   "Romeo and Juliet," I, iv, 97.

There is a very human impulse to create a world that doesn't exist, to ease the hurt we feel that this world is just not good enough—in fact, a vale of tears.

World-weary dissatisfaction with the sad state of the human condition is perhaps a valid excuse for indulging in fantasy. Naturally, artists have a license to do so, as the source of their creativity. But for most people after the age of fifteen, fantasy is a trap for the "idle brain." Even worse, it fosters our belief in magic and miracle and myth and legend, beguiling chimera that we could do without.

If you believe in fairies, you might just as well believe in ghosts. And if you believe that disembodied spirits wander the earth, you are well on your way to believing in an afterlife—each belief in the supernatural feeds another. This snare and delusion will divert your attention from the life you are living, its reality and finality. Each surrender to fantasy is an evasion of reality, a denial of death. If life after death is the same as life before death, you are in danger of living as though you were dead, and you might as well be.

The sin of fantasy is especially daunting to relationships. Because one person's fantasy is not necessarily another's, the world of fantasy is inward-looking, self-contained. Your daydream of winning a lottery and gambling at Monte Carlo does not require a partner or someone to share it with. It's a form of talking to oneself, much like masturbation.

If relationship is everything in life, it amounts to a total preoccupation, quest, experience, and adventure.

The wise person cultivates his or her relationships each waking hour of the day, in the same spirit with which Candide cultivated his garden—devoutly. Fantasy has no place in this equation, because a moment spent with "such stuff as dreams are made on" is a moment stolen from relationship. You owe it to the people you care about to get your head out of the clouds and stop pampering yourself with fancy and whim and fiction. As teenagers are fond of saying, get real.

WASTE

They say that a person is allocated, at birth, a finite number of heartbeats for a lifetime; when the heartbeats are expended, the person dies. If true, this means that each of us has been given a kind of bank account of life resources, and each of us is responsible for using them, conserving or squandering them at will. By analogy, we can think of a relationship as a living organism, with similar mechanisms to those of the human body, such as a power source that keeps it functioning. The logical extension of this analogy is that a relationship has a living history and is capable of growth or attrition, with the inevitability of eventual decay and demise.[1]

---

[1] The ominous outcome referred-to above is not pleasant to think about, and as a result we seldom explore its implications. The ideal relationship, let's face it, is one that ends in the simultaneous deaths of both partners. Of course, this rarely occurs and few relationships meet an ideal standard.

Thinking about a relationship in the way that we think about a human body encourages us to focus on what affects the welfare of the relationship positively or negatively. In general terms, this is the subject of the present chapter. In particular, what factors *adversely* affect the health of relationships? One of the most pernicious of the causes of decay I call "waste," for want of a better word.

What is wasteful in a relationship? The resources of any relationship include time and energy and trust and commitment and, of course, love; above all, perhaps, caring about the partner is the most nourishing. If any one of these resources is spent irresponsibly by one partner, the other is harmed because it diminishes the strength of the relationship. As an example, when a husband indulges himself in the Sin of Work, he depletes the amount of time that the relationship has left; if relationship is life, the theft of time is no less reprehensible than a waste of heartbeats.

The operative principle in the waste of life is risk. There are people who live by risk and people who avoid it whenever they can, but most would agree that the odds of winning are roughly equal to the odds of losing. Gamblers know this but believe that they can gain a foothold on the winning side and then "know when to quit." Nevertheless, the taking of a risk invites the possibility of waste.

The rationale for risk-taking is, naturally, to improve one's life, but the wish to improve one's life implies that the present life is deficient in some way; in short, the more risks you take, the less you value your life as it is. It follows that a compulsive gambler is the most miserable soul, but others take risks in equally self-punishing ways: examples are people who smoke or drink to excess, or indulge in other obsessional behavior such as driving recklessly. At risk is health and safety and, in the case of the suicidal person, life itself—the ultimate waste. The suicidal person who is religious can be more cavalier about risking death if he or she believes in life eternal, but the non-believer has no excuse; how can a rational person waste a life if he or she is not going anywhere when it's over?

The cynic might ask: "If I waste my life on a sport or a hobby or any other passion, so what? It's my life, isn't it?" That argument would be valid only if there were no waste of the resources of a relationship, therefore of life itself.

INDIFFERENCE

No relationship can withstand the destructive effects of indifference by one partner toward the other. It is fair to call Albert Camus the "poet of indifference," because he wrote so eloquently about how people show it, and so honestly about the wounds that it creates.[1] In simple terms, indifference is the opposite of empathy. In its extreme form, it is the absence of remorse. Consider what kind of person lacks the latter emotion: the psychopath

---

[1]   Chapter V. quotes Camus' famous insight into the reason for suicide.

wants to kill *someone*—without remorse; the sociopath wants to kill *anyone*—without remorse. When a person drops a bomb on a place where people live, there may be remorse, but to the identity of the victim there is nothing but indifference.

Being indifferent toward other human beings is the height of absurdity when one accepts that each of us shares 99.9% of his or her DNA with every other of the six billion people on this planet. That would be the same as being indifferent to yourself, a state that, no matter how you try, is virtually impossible to achieve. Many people attribute selflessness to Christ, who was the ideal person. To nearly everyone, being selfless is a mere abstraction. We are taught from the start to "look out for number one," and those who break the rule are shunned or locked away or burned at the stake.

The lessons that we are learning from the geneticists make a mockery of one person's feeling superior to another, not to mention prejudice or national pride or physical prowess or appearance. If you think about it, if people are all alike, when one person wins out in competition against others it must be sheer luck. One of the true blessings of traveling to other countries comes to you when you realize that people are the same all over the world, and that only an idiot would believe one culture or lifestyle to be better than another. In short, indifference toward another is living a lie.

Naturally, indifference is anathema to a relationship. Rarely is a mother indifferent to the needs of her child, but when she is, the child is in palpable danger. A husband who neglects his wife's feelings is not much of a husband and may find himself on the wrong side of the blanket. A leader who doesn't care about the needs of his followers may be taught a lesson by mutiny. We live for, and thrive on, the *regard* of others, and if that is denied us we feel rejected and alone. When Camus wrote "We are meant to live for others," he left unsaid the corollary: others are meant to live for us.

One of the strongest words in any language is the command to "pay attention." We demand it and we offer it. It's our only defense against the impulse not to care. In "Death of a Salesman," the wife of Willy Loman, standing by his grave, reminds us ". . . attention must be paid . . . attention, attention must be finally paid to such a person."

THE SEVENTH SIN

Worse than any of the follies and foibles of everyday life that are described above is what you and I have done in these pages, writing and reading, We have had the chutzpah to pretend that we haven't felt any of those feelings or performed any of those acts. We have chosen to believe that we are not guilty of any of them, but others are. With the smugness of the true voyeur, who sees but is not seen, we have frowned and laughed at those lesser souls who waste their lives or wreck relationships by jealousy or fantasy or deceit. In our self-righteousness, we have cast the first stone at those who live only to work or who poison the love of others through indifference. In our conceit, we have looked down our noses at people who have failed in their relationships, merely because we know why relationships fail. Feeling "holier than thou" in this way blinds us to danger signs in our own interactions with others. Worse than conceit is a false conceit, in which we fool *ourselves*: "To thine own self be true."

Organized religion has many flaws (See Chapter XV.), not the least of which are mass hysteria and delusions of immortality, but some religious rites have practical benefit. For instance, the cleansing rituals of the Catholic confession and the Jewish *kol nidrei* are useful exercises that encourage people to "own up" to their transgressions. Folk wisdom holds that "confession is good for the soul"; that may be, but it is even better for relationships, which thrive on honesty. If we admit our jealousy, deceit, indifference, and other crimes of the heart, we shall have taken a step nearer to apologizing for them, and may one day be forgiven in return.

When we begin to think seriously about relationship being the touchstone to understanding our lives, we begin casting obligation and sentiments in a new light. The reader may have noticed that the values described here serve not Divine Providence but flesh-and-blood persons. They do not extol virtues like piety or reverence or prudence or charity or humility or unquestioning faith. As varieties of human experience, these traits and behaviors are their own rewards. Nevertheless, they cannot alone or in combination meet the vital, quotidian needs of a relationship between two people. What better proof can there be that the standard moral imperatives are obsolete today? If we do not create a new ethic for our time, how can we be sure that we have left the Middle Ages far behind?

The seven lively sins are exemplars of relationship taboos. The kinds of pressures that they represent threaten the infrastructure of a relationship. Turned inside-out, they show the way to what must be done to preserve and enhance the relationships we have formed:

- tell the truth
- work less
- indulge less in wishful thinking
- take fewer chances with your life
- be less critical of others
- trust more
- care more

Platitudes such as these will remind you of the advice of the self-improvement guru who wants you to feel better about yourself—more confident, more popular, richer, etc. Even so, their true value lies elsewhere, because they are based on giving, not taking. Their purpose is not to build ego-strength but to nourish relationships. Doing these things will strengthen your bond with another person—guaranteed.

Finally, if the DNA of human beings is essentially interchangeable one-to-another, everything that is special about the people in your life came to you by luck. And, the most important person in your life might have been anyone. The fact that it isn't, that this incomparable person among six billion is your partner in your orbit around the sun, is as close as we come to Destiny.

VIII

Why We Die

"Life is full of suffering."

—Siddharta Gautama, the Buddha

"Mother died today, or maybe it was yesterday."

—Albert Camus: first line of *L'Étranger*

It never made sense to me to reflect that, after the great labors of God or the Life Force or X to make life, the same power would decide to destroy it. Of course, this power is indifferent to the death of one particular person or animal or plant, but why should that one life end, only to be replaced by another? That some lives should be canceled merely that others may take their places is absurd—the logic does not hold. Instead of a Chain of Being, there could be a single unbroken link, or one for each of life's three kingdoms. Because those plants or animals or people would not change, there would be no need for evolution, which is simply a blueprint for change. Reproduction would not be necessary if there were no members of a species needing to be replaced.

Death teaches life everything. When I wrote that, in *The Meaning of Life*, I meant it literally, because we cannot see life plainly without contemplating its negation—life's reciprocal. In that context, death gives a value for life: the specter of death, looming before each of us every day, leads us to cherish what we have, in peril of losing it. If death did not exist, we would have to invent it.

The foregoing, however worth thinking about, does not answer the question of why the Creator (God, Life Force, or X) decided that death would serve *its* purpose. Consider the possibility that, originally, life was to go on indefinitely; but, in the process of creating life it was learned that only the giant sequoias could begin to fulfill that requirement. In fact, Man would be among the least of the animals when it comes to longevity—by contrast with parrots, tortoises, *et al.* If creatures cannot live forever, they might instead be permitted to live well. But, if life is truly "full of suffering," how could the Creator be so cruel?

We die because the suffering must end. In this, we can recognize the Creator's greatest gift to us: having given us flesh that can only decay in an existence that, after a while, declines in pleasure with each passing day, we are granted release by the same force that made us—Hamlet's "surcease from sorrow." The Creator, if not all-powerful, has a merciful side.

Among those who choose death as a means to an end are the suicides, the vast majority of whom do it to punish another person. Then there are the martyrs, who court death because it would prove the righteousness of a cause, or have been promised admittance at the gates of eternal life. For any petty tyrant, unsure of his or her place in history, the martyr's death is a necessity, truly "a consummation devoutly to be wished." One such, Yasser Arafat, clearly understood this when he told the press "They want me either under arrest or in exile or dead, but I am telling them I prefer to be martyred." In dramatic form, this was the theme of Camus' play "Caligula." In the play, the Roman Emperor commits the most despicable acts, one after the other, and makes powerful enemies. Finally, he *forces* the enemies to kill him, thus achieving his martyrdom. Camus described his play as "the story of a superior suicide." It was superior because Caligula didn't even have to kill himself, since others were willing to do it for him. To the end, he was the master of his fate, and the fact that his killers would be branded assassins was the cream of the jest.

While few of us crave martyrdom, we think a lot about death, pondering what dying might feel like and what our death could mean. Poets have expressed these thoughts for us, often through the metaphor of the dream. Perhaps Shakespeare's was the most eloquent:

> To die: to sleep;
> No more; and by a sleep to say we end
> The heart-ache and the thousand natural shocks
> That flesh is heir to . . .
> ("Hamlet," III, 1)

This idea of the "sleep of death," certainly not original to Shakespeare, suggests that not only do we dwell on thoughts of death, we experience a form of dying each night when we close our eyes and let consciousness fade.

It may be that the Creator gave us sleep as a rehearsal for dying. If we live out the proverbial "three score and ten" years, we shall have experienced more than 25,000 nights of seeking—if not always finding—sleep. The poet said that we sleep to "knit up the ravelled sleeve of care"; to rest the body, you may say. But it could be motivated by sheer audacity. For instance, if I "let myself die" in this way, will not my satisfaction be great when I awaken in the morning? If life is a test, then we prove our merit with each day's rising. When we surrender to sleep, we reaffirm our trust in whoever is our god. We sleep to remind us that we die. Each awakening is a resurrection.

How we die is another matter. Our only insight comes when we observe someone else's misfortune, in proximity to the final events. We watch, detached, feel sorry, curse the fates, and prepare ourselves for what life will expect of *us* after the dying person is gone. And because few of us have an experience like this, most of us have no more knowledge of dying than of exploring the moon. Those who have had "near death" experiences give conflicting accounts of what it felt like, probably based on their fantasies of what it might feel like. This blind-spot in our thinking is hard to understand, because even if we believe the gurus who tell us that we "die a little" each day, we seldom act as though we believe it.

If we knew a man who was dying, what would we say to him if we knew he could hear us? If an apology were warranted, could we offer one? If forgiveness were sought, could we grant it? What words would convey how much we expect to be grieving? If we desire his death, could we summon the strength not to let him know? Would we have the empathy to know how we would feel if it was our turn to be lying there, *in extremis?* Every experience is a lesson for something to come, and what is there to be learned from another man's death?

Each death is a loss to some who remain: e.g., a venerable professor dies in his sleep, alone, and the journal of his scholarly field prints an obituary; each of his students who reads it is flooded with memories, happy or sad, of that place and that person and oneself as one was at that time. Reading the obituary unites those people for a moment, and even though they do not share the same emotion, they are collectively moved just the same.

We are so caught-up in the business of staying alive that the death of a person whom we know, after our denial and shock, is felt as a threat to us personally: "Am I like her?"; "Is that the way I'll go?"; "Do I look as run-down as he did?" We check ourselves out to assess if we are more robust than the acquaintance was. For many people past the age of forty, this turns out to be a morbid assessment, because we are greeted each morning by a pain somewhere. Here is proof of our deepest fear, namely that our bodies are the worst enemies we shall ever know.

How we die a "natural death" is absurdly simple—although a more complex process is hardly preferable. Loss of power is followed by loss of well-being, and the loss of one organ's functioning implies that another will soon shut down as well. When a "critical mass" of shut-down organs occurs, the enterprise is functionally bankrupt. We die because not enough organs can carry on. Their collective will is gone. Absent further resistance, the "mortal coil" loosens its grip and the suffering intensifies until merciful death gives deliverance.

IX

Saying Goodbye

We shall go on living, Uncle Vanya. We shall live through a long, long chain of days and endless evenings; we shall patiently bear the trials fate sends us; we'll work for others, now and in our old age, without ever knowing rest, and when our time comes, we shall die submissively; and there, beyond the grave, we shall say that we have suffered, that we have wept, and have known bitterness, and God will have pity on us; and you and I, Uncle, dear Uncle . . . shall rest. I have faith, Uncle, I have fervent, passionate faith . . . We shall rest!

     —Anton Chekhov, "Uncle Vanya"

Your death was old already when your life began.

     —Rainer Maria Rilke, "Requiem"

They say that the Chinese character for our word "crisis" is a combination of the characters that represent two other words, "danger" and "opportunity." A crisis may well expose the person to danger of some kind, but mature reflection may reveal a blessing in disguise. And if dying qualifies as the ultimate danger, it follows that dying offers the ultimate opportunity. Naturally, this is a chance to "set one's house in order," but on a grander scale it is an opportunity to stage-manage one's exit from the human comedy, to plan a farewell address before the final curtain. My father died of a stroke when he was 69, and by all accounts had no warning that the end had come. Many people haven't the slightest premonition of it either, and these unfortunates will be denied the benefits of the demise I am advocating here.

Many people don't plan for their dying because they see it not as an exit but as an entrance. They will be admitted at the Pearly Gates and sing with the Choir Celestial. Some are so eager to get where they think they are going that they can't be bothered by pleasantries as they edge toward the door—they can't wait. This rationale is echoed by their survivors, who announce their deaths with terse optimism; e.g., the loved-one:

- began everlasting life
- went to Heaven peacefully in her sleep
- entered into Eternal Life
- went home to be with the Lord
- entered into Eternal Rest
- was received into the arms of our Lord

These sentiments, although genuine, emphasize what the deceased is doing or will soon be doing, as opposed to what he or she left behind in life—a project just begun or completed—or the acknowledgement of a lifetime's achievements. Obituaries invariably lack an account of the person's last words or even offer a point of view on that life's meaning. This is usually because the person who died, struck suddenly by timidity, made no statement at the end. Very few follow the advice of Dylan Thomas to "rage, rage against the dying of the light." They accept the danger but miss the opportunity.

As the quotation from Rilke reminds us, we are dying from the moment when we are conceived. To the cynic among us, the human being is a dying machine. To the more sanguine, dying is as natural a function as breathing, as programmed to end life as it was to begin—when aided by the slap of an attending nurse. Some people show their awareness of this process by planning their funerals in advance, choosing caskets, etc. When they do that, in a sense they have started saying goodbye to their loved-ones, at least those who know about the preparations. This planning signifies that the person has felt strong intimations of mortality and has taken them to heart. Having been humiliated often enough in life, a person cannot abide the thought of humiliation in death. The wish for a "decent burial" or its equivalent is universal.

In the theater, the Curtain Call, in which the actors and actresses approach the footlights and take their bows, is choreographed and rehearsed in advance. In the case of a person who is dying, this preparation might include a visit to the gravesite accompanied by loved-ones. Having done that, it would be natural to turn one's attention to rehearsing and refining the final scene. Not many people do this. Dying is so much associated with the pain and exhaustion of fatal illness that, for many people, thinking about it beforehand is out of the question. Yet the death scene will be etched in the memories of those who witness it, and recounted and re-enacted over and over for the benefit of those who were not there. Why should it not be as joyous an occasion as, say, a wedding? A wake is intended to give the survivors as much "closure" to their experience of a death as possible. Could there not be a wake *before the fact*, in which the moribund person is the star of the show? It has been done. It gives the man or woman a forum for saying goodbye.

Naturally, many people say goodbye by the simple act of leaving a will, in which they identify certain key relationships and give them a last appraisal—favorable or unfavorable—by the terms of their bequests. For instance, a person might send a message like one of these:

> To my inveterate jerk of a brother, I leave the money that you owe me, a debt which has, I believe, hastened my death. This means, you bastard, that YOU WON.

> To my unfaithful wife I leave, if she will be patient, a most unpleasant smell.

Other wills normally contain far more endearing messages than those, but when they are read aloud in an office by a lawyer seated behind a desk, they leave a certain humanity to be desired. Coldly frank, they lack the passion of an interaction in which the speaker is on a deathbed and the other *must listen*. Whether for celebration or condemnation, a last will and testament is too little and too late.

The value of taking whatever opportunity one has to say goodbye face-to-face, lies in its being a last chance to:

1. give thanks to someone;
2. right a wrong;
3. make a final point;
4. extract a promise from someone;
5. scorn an enemy;
6. have "the last laugh";
7. offer an apology;
8. reveal a secret;
9. complete a project;
10. speak the unspeakable at last.

There are tasks such as these that remain among the "unfinished business" of anyone's life, and for those who are lucky enough to have time for them, they are well worth accomplishing.

A common denominator in most of these farewell declarations, whether tender or harsh, is that they are addressed to a dying relationship. If life is relationship, they can give final meaning to a life. And when the partner replies to them or acknowledges them in some way, he or she adds meaning to both lives. The guiding principle is to make every moment count—even this one. When E. M. Forster wrote his famous advice, "Only connect," he must have meant: if it's the last thing you do.

X

Hell Is Over

Hell is oneself.

> —T. S. Eliot, "The Cocktail Party"

Hell is other people.

> —Jean-Paul Sartre, "No Exit"

These conflicting views of the nature of Hell may reflect the difference between being born in Paris and being born in St. Louis, Missouri. Nevertheless, if the term "hell" is meant as a metaphor for human misery, being alone might be the worst torture a person could endure; and, being in a pathological relationship could be equally destructive. Indeed, you may be your own worst enemy (Eliot) or you may be someone's victim (Sartre), but your torture will be administered in this life, not after it.

No thinking person believes in Hell anymore, and the net result is perpetual freedom or, if you will, total license. The idea of a repository of souls where retribution is meted out for earthly sins is as quaint as the notion that aliens are hovering about in UFOs. The bankruptcy of belief in an Inferno of fire and brimstone begs the conceit that, if no one catches you, you can get away with anything. How this paradigm shift in Western values will alter the mores of our civilization is not yet determined, but the universality of this cynicism marks at least half of the religious teachings of our time as hypocrisy. This pervasive influence on our cultural standards is, in sum, far greater even than those mega-cynics, Eliot and Sartre, could have imagined.

The concept of Hell has had many seasons, coming and going on the wings of myth. The ancient Egyptians, for example, had no need of a Hell where sins would be punished and the greater the sin the more severe the punishment. They believed that, when a person dies, he or she is judged according to his or her earthly deeds; this rite was described by Parrinder:

. . . everyone after death would face a 'weighing of the heart' . . . There are many representations and texts dealing with the idea. In one of the scales a symbol of Maat (Truth) is shown; in the other is the heart of the deceased, and if his virtues enabled him to achieve a balance with Truth, then the verdict was favorable and eternal happiness was secured. If not, a monster called the 'Devourer of the Dead' was waiting to destroy the condemned one.[1]

As the Egyptians saw it, the virtuous would live after death while the sinful would merely cease to exist. Theirs were not necessarily vengeful gods.

The Greeks, through their master mythmaker, Homer, saw Hell (in his word, "Hades") as " . . . a place of gloom but not necessarily a place of punishment and torture."[2] Life after death for the guilty could occur, but it would not be pleasant. Edith Hamilton wrote:

In Homer the underworld is vague, a shadowy place inhabited by shadows. Nothing is real there. The ghosts' existence, if it can be called that, is like a miserable dream.[3]

---

[1]   Parrinder, G. (Ed.) *World Religions: From Ancient History to the Present* (1971), New York: Facts on File Publications, p. 145.

[2]   Evans, I. H. (Ed.) *Brewer's Dictionary of Phrase and Fable*, (1981), New York: Harper & Row, p. 519.

[3]   Hamilton, E. *Mythology* (1942), Boston: Little, Brown, pp. 42, 43.

It was the Romans who bequeathed to us our familiar notion of a Hell; according to Hamilton:

> The later poets define the world of the dead more and more clearly as the place where the wicked are punished and the good rewarded. In the Roman poet Virgil this idea is presented in great detail . . . all the torments of the one class and the joys of the other are described at length.[1]

Since Virgil lived and died before the birth of Christ, it is reasonable to conclude that the dominant culture of Rome provided the basic imagery of Hell to Christianity (if not to Judaism). So, for two thousand years, we have been forced to cope with feverish imaginings such as those of Dante and Milton, and wrestle with the temptations of Satan and Beelzebub to save our souls.

There is no sense in arguing with a Jesuit or a Fundamentalist or, for that matter, with a Muslim, about what punishment awaits a sinful person after death—chiefly because, in their heart of hearts, they don't believe it anyway. Unable to exert a negative force, not even symbolically, religion cannot regulate human behavior. And if religion lacks the power to deter human beings from committing hurtful or destructive acts, what good is religion? Without a supernatural deterrent to evil, religion can offer only beatitudes.

---

[1]   Hamilton, *op. cit.*, p. 43.

When people lose their fear of Hell, they lose their need for Heaven. If everyone is equally good, the distinction of who belongs where after death becomes moot. Similarly, the question of whether an act is virtuous or sinful is irrelevant, because there is no reward for the former and no retribution for the latter. The Church, which for Dostoevsky ruled by "miracle, mystery, and authority," has lost its authority. The mantra becomes "If it feels good, do it," and if others are offended one has only to answer to a secular court. Of course, something must emerge to control the excesses of behavior that, if not deterred, can delay or reverse the march of civilization. Finding an answer to that question will be the subject of chapters to follow.

XI

There Is No Hope

Hope is the mother of fools.

—Polish saying

Just stop lying about yourself and kidding yourself
about tomorrows . . . it will be worth it to you in
the end, after you're rid of the damned guilt that
makes you lie to yourselves you're something you're
not, and the remorse that nags at you and makes you
hide behind lousy pipe dreams . . . they're the things
that really poison and ruin a guy's life and keep him
from finding any peace.

—Eugene O'Neill, "The Iceman Cometh"

When Pandora opened that famous box and let loose upon the world all its evils, only Hope remained inside the box as a form of consolation. Trying to prove that this was a blessing or a booby prize is not worth doing if hope is a chimera—doesn't exist. Whether fanciful illusion or pathetic delusion, hope is ever-present in our lives if we pay attention to people's use of the term; we hear "I hope" nearly as often as "I want" or "I think," with about the same awareness of what is being said by the one who is saying it. What, then, does a person mean by "I hope you're feeling better" or "I hope to visit the South of France this summer" or "I hope I'm right about this"?

"Hope" is a word that serves to express our sense that something may be amiss, and that things might not turn out as well as we would like (When someone tells you "good luck," it may be that the person thinks you need it.). It can be used as a pleasantry (as in "hope you're feeling better"), as wish-fulfillment fantasy ("hope to visit the South of France"), or to hedge a bet ("hope I'm right"). It acknowledges the tendency of life to dash expectations and the fallibility of prediction. In that regard, it reflects a sentiment that, although genuinely human, is thoroughly self-defeating.

Based on the folk notion that "wishing will make it so," hoping represents a pathological mode of thought that mental health professionals call "reistic" (from "reify," c.f. *Oxford Dictionary*: "convert mentally into a thing"). Reistic thinking is a symptom of schizophrenia in its extreme usage and, when firmly established as a habit, is often impervious to treatment. If a man wants to be Napoleon, he *becomes*

Napoleon and will not be talked out of it. In short, this is the creation of reality, and it cannot be undone by realistic means. It does no good to tell the man that Napoleon has been dead since 1821. A part of his mind knows that he is not Napoleon, but another part insists that his version of reality is just as good as yours; and what right do you have to tell him who to be? This is the tyranny of hoping and other species of self-deception: the belief that one's own needs, if expressed as a hope, will take precedence not only over the needs of others but over natural laws. "I hope it won't rain" epitomizes this solipsism.

If hope is the mother of fools, prayer is her demented cousin. To pray is to ask for help in reaching a wished-for outcome. It is sent up in the form of an exhortation or entreaty or plea. And while hoping does not require speech nor even needs to be put into words, prayer is an attempt at communication: it sends a message to an imagined object that is assumed to be listening. While hoping is a feeling, prayer is a behavior aimed at or toward a presumed audience, e.g., "Grant him a safe journey" or "Please let him forgive me" or "Please help me show her how much I love her." The fact that none of us believes that someone or something will "hear" our prayer does not deter us from composing it in our minds, phrasing it, and even giving voice to it in church or wherever the social conventions will accept it.

What is accepted is a sort of communal autism, in which one can make any statement, however absurd, and not be held accountable for it, possibly even praised for its selflessness. If I pray, for example, that our troops will return safely from wherever our warlike nature has taken us now, it is far more acceptable than if I pray for snow in the Sierras so that I may go skiing. Therefore, there are good prayers and not-so-good prayers, depending on context, as well as ritual prayers such as "Hail Mary, full of grace," or "If I should die before I wake, I pray the Lord my soul will take," which we say by rote so thoughtlessly that their meaning has been lost. The prayer, then, entails talking-to-oneself that is essentially pathological but is excused for its piety. In theory, the more a person asks for in prayer, the more that person is considered devout. Praying is its own reward.

The impracticality of this seemingly harmless approach to problem-solving is exemplified by the familiar telecast in which a public vigil is held to mourn the death of a youth who was murdered in the street by an ostensible random act of violence. Well-meaning people, carrying candles and singing hymns, march along and proudly display their placards that say "Stop the violence NOW" or "Pray for peace." These are righteous people whose efforts are admirable, but the efforts divert their attention away from the causes of violence in their milieu of abuse and ignorance and guns. In a month or two, there will be another murder followed by more songs and placards and prayers. The violent way of life is their way of life, and change from within is their only prospect for a non-violent community. They must change it in the homes, not in the streets. Peace is learned at the dinner table.

Prayer derives its power from the same source as superstition, which depends upon the naive notion that events occurring closely together are causally connected in some way. Indeed, two events may be related by the fact that they occurred in close proximity of time or place or both, but that does not necessarily mean that the one event caused the other. This susceptibility to superstition can affect people in hurtful ways; for example, a man who is injured in a car accident may, later on, blame himself for having been driving his car in that place on that day, when his doing so and the accident were completely coincidental. If he has taken on himself a lot of undeserved guilt, he may be reluctant to drive for a while, or at least may avoid driving on that highway. This kind of behavior is fueled by fear, but its source is irrational thinking. When a human act is based on superstition, it cannot be explained by logical means. If a blind man, restored to sight, saw a crowd of people supplicating themselves in prayer, he might well ask "What are they afraid of now?" In sum, prayer is a waste of breath.

XII

Philosophy for the Third Millennium

The world is everything that is the case . . . Whereof
one cannot speak, thereof one must be silent.
    —Ludwig Wittgenstein, first and last lines of
                    Tractatus Logico-Philosophicus

Midway in our life's journey, I went astray from the
straight road and woke to find myself alone in a dark
wood. How shall I say what wood that was! I never
saw so drear, so rank, so arduous a wilderness!
    —Dante Alighieri, first line of *Inferno*

If, in your travels, you wander into the realm of Philosophy in our time, you will find yourself in a dark wood indeed. Philosophy today has lost its voice. It has nothing to inform us about, nothing to wish for us. Moreover, no one is listening. No political leader is a philosopher and none would turn to a philosopher for advice on policy or governance. Decisions about education, health, poverty, crime, cultural differences, religious tolerance, the environment, business practices, quality of life, or even the future of our civilization are made without the aid of philosophical discourse of any serious kind.

How did this happen to a once-revered intellectual discipline? It is not enough to say that philistinism rules our world, although that is certainly true, but ideas are still universally sought, and thinking-things-through to solve problems is still preferred to the impulsive acting-out of the booboisie. The sea change that marks the Twentieth Century has meant that philosophers are no longer conceiving those ideas or thinking those thoughts.

Philosophy became diverted from its mission and its influence on Western culture consequently declined for various reasons, some of which can be attributed to bad luck. In France, for example, war and the aftermath of war dominated the Forties and Fifties. During the war, both Sartre and Camus were caught up in the question of how much they owed to the Resistance; before and after the war, both tried to decide how much they owed to Communism. Philosophy in England may have been propelled into its decline by Russell and Whitehead's

Principia Mathematica, a book which implied that the wisdom of Kant and Hume and Locke—not to mention Socrates, Plato, and Aristotle—could be reduced to a set of equations.[1] The publication, in 1922, of Wittgenstein's oracular tautologies, of which two of the silliest are quoted above, hastened a descent from which British Philosophy has never recovered. American Philosophy, never a hardy child, was infected with a strain of the British "linguistic philosophy" and, for lack of nourishment, failed to thrive. German intellectual life in general was made sclerotic by the century's two world wars; its most well-known philosopher, Heidegger, was defeated by his own Nazism.

In the Third Millennium, this bankrupt field of inquiry must find a new *raison d'etre*. This can be accomplished by (1) choosing new subjects for inquiry; (2) returning to subjects long discarded; or, (3) adopting new methods of inquiry. Philosophers in the Third Millennium will take one of those paths, as will be shown in chapters to follow. But first, who is a philosopher? I use the term to refer to anyone who thinks things through, there being no limit

---

[1]   Example: "A sentence like 'I met a man' is analyzed as follows: 'There is some x such that x is human and I met x.' The analysis shows that what corresponds to 'a' has become 'there is some x such that' and it attaches to the propositional function 'x is human and I met x.'" Sainsbury, R.M., "Russell, Bertrand," Entry in Honderich, T. (Ed.) *The Oxford Companion to Philosophy* (1995) Oxford: Oxford University Press, p. 782.

to thought in its depth. The philosopher thinks to find the solution to a problem, but so does, for example, the engineer. More than the engineer, the philosopher, along the way to a solution, thinks about why the problem exists and why the solution has been so elusive until now. What other similar problems can possibly be solved by the same means of approach? The philosopher also asks what the consequences might be if the problem in question were never solved.

The only resources on which a philosopher can rely are the thoroughness and daring of his or her thinking. By "daring" is meant a willingness to think thoughts that no one has previously thought, and an openness to holding these thoughts out to others for criticism. If I say, for instance, that prayer is useless, I must be prepared to accept proof of the counterargument, namely that prayer has benefit. Perhaps I can accept a modification such as this: prayer serves a useful purpose if the sound of one's voice (outward or inward) in prayer comforts the person who prays, because he or she feels that as much as possible is being done to solve a problem. In that way, the act of praying has value in and of itself, although it has no power to solve the problem. The new Philosophy that I propose in this book follows closely this example, in which reason is tempered by humanity. It is not enough for the philosopher merely to cover a blackboard with the symbols of mathematical logic; a philosopher must be a person first and a philosopher second. Unfortunately, some who are called philosophers and have views *about* life, are not *in* life. One such is the current Dalai Lama, who is said to have become the "divine" ruler of Tibet through reincarnation. He writes of the meaning of life while not being *in* life: as far as is known, he doesn't drive a car.

Whatever course Philosophy will take in coming years, it must rise above its fascination with subjects like the Mind-Body Question or the contents of consciousness or the theory of knowledge ("What do we know and how do we know it?"). These inquiries must be discarded in favor of questions that pertain to everyday life. Philosophers must give advice, clarify dilemmas, help people cope. They must speak to the common man without condescension, in terms of the present day and the listener's place in the world. In short, Philosophy must be *relevant*, something it hasn't been in a hundred years.

XIII

The Way Out of the Wood

. . . we are all often faced with moral questions . . . most of us, when we have to answer these questions, do some thinking about them. It will be generally agreed that this kind of thinking . . . can be done well or badly. It is the task of moral philosophy to help us do it better . . . We want the moral philosopher to help us do our moral thinking more rationally.

—R.M. Hare, *Moral Thinking*

More than half a century ago, the Oxford philosopher R. M. Hare set out, in *The Language of Morals* (1952) a view of the role of philosopher as an arbiter of societal values. Hare's concept of "prescriptivism" meant that rational judgments about people's conduct could be expressed in "prescriptions" that would guide moral choices. At that time, Hare's was in many ways a voice crying in the wilderness, because in the Fifties existentialism was in vogue in France, and in England and America the linguistic philosophers held sway. The former might have dismissed Hare's moral philosophy as "not worth it" because the universe is absurd; the latter group might have said "It's none of your business" because they, themselves, saw ethical principles as incapable of proof. By any standard, Hare's work was ignored or unappreciated, and at his death in 2002 he was the forgotten man of British Philosophy.

While it is true that a moral prescription is not subject to proof, mathematical or scientific, people yearn for signposts that lead to right conduct. In essence, they need to be told, however gently, what it would be best for them to do. The Bible contains a thousand prescriptions for human behavior, and folk wisdom is never at a loss for words to live by. We seem to have an unquenchable thirst for guidance, and we take it where we can find it. Meanwhile, Philosophy is silent and turns its face away.

To find a new Philosophy for the Third Millennium is a task involving repudiation of its recent past. In review, not only has Philosophy nothing in common with linguistics, it is not the study of ideas nor is it an analysis of the nature of thought. If this discipline is to have any influence on the world it describes or the events it explains, it must first tell what is right and wrong about the world. It properly dwells in morality—not metaphysics; in ethical principles—not structures of language; in passion—not logic. The role of the philosopher is to set a course for human life, as it could be lived were reason guiding behavior. The ultimate object of philosophical research is the formulation of values for an era of civilization. As that era merges with another, Philosophy must change: manners and mores are unique to place and time, and Philosophy owes to every generation a sensitivity to the aims and pressures of each era respectively. Shooting a horse for food is unacceptable behavior except, perhaps, in time of famine. Naturally, this convention is not followed slavishly in every country but, in most countries, horses are safe. This is an example of a taboo that has evolved, that is widely acknowledged, and is not likely ever to be rescinded.

Since time began, human behavior has been fundamentally good or evil. The task of Philosophy is to assign each act a place on the continuum between those extremes. In that sense, judgment is the soul of Philosophy, but it is not its function to pass judgment on any person; instead, judgment is reserved for the act itself, as opposed to the act's alternatives, thereby giving people rational choices. In specific instances, lawmakers weigh the positive or negative values of acts before writing laws to permit or prohibit them, and judges judge the choices after they are made. But a philosopher is not fettered by the political motives of lawmakers or the prejudices of judges, or even the biases of religion. A timely example is the issue of abortion in the United States: the law makes it legal, but the political-religious debate rages on. A philosopher stands above religious cant and has no political agenda (Plato's concept of the philosopher king is misguided; philosophers are the least likely kings.). The philosopher's task, in relation to abortion, is to take up controversial questions such as "When does life begin?" and "When does life become meaningful?" and, ultimately, "What is life?"

Other, similar issues arise in the case of euthanasia or its twin, "assisted suicide." The relevant philosophical questions range from "When is life no longer worth living?" to "What should a life accomplish?" to "How does a person know that he or she has gotten enough out of life?" To pass a law permitting the deliberate termination of a life would be irresponsible, if those subjects were not assiduously thought-through.

The field of medical ethics and the related discipline of bioethics are the closest equivalents to true philosophical inquiry that exist today. The concept of triage, according to which the most severly ill person receives the first care, is a moral paradigm. Medical ethicists ask, for example, whether it is proper to create life by cloning or artificial insemination, or what criteria should apply to giving a vital organ transplant to one person as opposed to another, when organs for transplantation are scarce. "Who lives?" is the question here, opening the door to questions such as "Can one person's life be more valuable than someone else's?" and "Who decides?" These are essentially philosophical conundrums and, although they arise in a medical context, their study is not the province of medical science. The role of Philosophy is to propose solutions to these problems and for physicians to dispose. The Hippocratic Oath, whose theme is best expressed by the Latin phrase *Primum, non nocere* (Above all, do no harm.) provides insufficient guidance for dealing with these issues, because the problems themselves originate in discoveries that could not have been foreseen in ancient Greece.

These practicalities aside, the most valuable aspect of ethics in medicine is not what it accomplishes—saving a life that might otherwise be lost—but what it reveals. It brings us nearer to the supreme mystery of the meaning of death. A man whose liver is about to shut down completely receives our deepest sympathy and the first available sound liver. We don't ask whether or not the person was a thief or beat his wife or was some other species of villain. We try to find a liver for him first, although we may ask questions about his character later. His eligibility is established solely by his being on the brink of death. This implies that we take everyone's death as a personal affront—a punishment neither the deceased nor we, the living, deserved. Our efforts to preserve life by delaying death extend to any life, any death.

To review, Philosophy exists to tell people not what to do, but what they should do. This, of course, is an arbitrary choice of one alternative in the classic dichotomy of "is" versus "ought." This choice heralds the return of the discipline to its role in the exploration of moral pathways. Its true subject, conduct, is real and observable, and its object is to prescribe behavioral rules that any person could follow.

In the Third Millennium, a time when the influence of the church (any church) is waning, secular values prevail. Nietzsche said that "God is dead" and, in the oft-told joke, God said "Nietzsche is dead." If both God and Nietzsche are dead, we are free to look at religious teachings in a new light. An example is that of the Golden Rule: should we love our neighbors as ourselves?; if so, why? What shades of meaning lie beneath the shibboleth "Thou shalt not kill"? In his play, "The Time of Your Life," William Saroyan wrote: "When the time comes to kill, kill and have no regrets." Precisely what he meant by that is not clear, and few would agree with it, but it is a moral prescription and its implications are worth exploring. The reflection that it inspires is uniquely philosophical.

Is it possible for a philosopher to alter the course of history or to have an impact on world events? Rarely, you would say, but consider this: imagine that, in China in the Ch'in Dynasty (221-206 B.C.), the emperor had told the alchemists and engineers who invented gunpowder that the invention should be suppressed, and the knowledge that led to its creation destroyed; would the world, for some time thereafter, have been a safer place? Or suppose our friend Nietzsche had written a forceful letter in 1867 to Alfred Nobel in Sweden, persuading him to destroy the formula for dynamite, on grounds that it would ultimately be more harm to people than help. Foreseeing contingencies such as these does not require a philosopher, but the person who foresees them will have a philosophical cast of mind. He or she may ask "What is the value of blowing something to pieces?" or "Why do we want to shoot something?" Any answer on the order of "to win a war," for example, begs the questions "Why do we need wars?" and "Why do we need to win something?," and so on into the labyrinth where we encounter the Minotaur who guards the *questions that are not to be asked.*

The moralist judges, and no earthly subject is immune to judgment. The philosopher needs only the courage of his or her convictions, leavened by the awareness that, in proposing what is right or wrong, it is as easy to be wrong as right. The moralist is holier than no one, but can only claim to have given more thought to moral issues than other people, including theologians, whose thinking is encumbered by Holy Writ. The first obligation of a philosopher is to have no obligations—no religious ties, no political agenda, no allegiance to any movement or ideology or cause. Only in this way can he or she ask the best questions. And even though this person may be personally incapable of living by the principles proposed, he or she must trust that the principles are better than others to live by, and that those who follow them will live fulfilled lives.

No philosophy has merit that does not tell us what in our world is meritorious, nor is worthy that does not say what is worth doing with our lives. This is the way out of the dark wood.

XIV

An Essay on Morals

A time will come when everyone will know what all this is for, why there is all this suffering, and there will be no mysteries; but meanwhile, we must live . . . it seems as if just a little more and we shall know why we live, why we suffer . . . If only we knew, if only we knew!

—Anton Chekhov, "The Three Sisters"

Why we were brought into the world in the first place only to suffer and die is an area of research in which much remains to be done.

—Ian Frazier, "Researchers Say"

At the core of human existence is relationship. Any prescription for conduct that leads to a better quality of life enhances a person's relationships. Any prescription that improves a relationship enriches a person's life.

A moral philosophy can have no relevance for people in general unless its foundation is the meaning of life. That a person's life is relationship-bound and relationship-driven is the starting-point for any set of guidelines designed to regulate behavior. Any systematic regimen of DOs and DON'Ts must consider the context of every person's relationships with others. This differs from our perspective on laws, for example, that we are obliged to obey as individuals or be held accountable as individuals, because laws are believed to reflect the will of society. In a relationship, our first obligation is to the other person, on behalf of the relationship. Then what do we owe God, the company we work for, the community, our State or Nation, our culture, civilization, mankind, the human race? Relatively speaking, we owe nothing. What debts we have are debts to other people.

The core relationships of our lives are with loved-ones in the immediate family and the family of origin, those whom we call friends, a few neighbors, some co-workers, and our household pets. Any ethic proposed to guide people to right conduct begins within this matrix and then radiates outward to acquaintances, the extended family, colleagues, neighbors, and so on. If we are true to those who are closest, we shall be true to the rest.

This transition to a new foundation for values requires a fresh perspective on each person's unique role in the world. For as long as they have thought about this, people have built belief systems either on pantheism (everything is god and god is everything) or polytheism (there are many gods) or monotheism such as that of Judaism or Islam or the Christian faith. In most instances, the person's destiny rests on how well he or she pleases the operative god(s). Such devotion here, of course, is intended to secure admittance to a life hereafter. This goal, we are told, is shared with the Neanderthals of 100,000 years ago, who placed food in the graves of the departed so that they would not go hungry in the afterlife.

If some miracle of psychotropic medication could remove delusions like these from our consciousness, we would need to worship no god. Then, if we decided to rid ourselves of the worship of money or power or fame or the rest of the false gods, we would worship nothing. Since worship relies on belief and belief is subservient to will, we could force ourselves to overcome the habit. The first evolutionary advance of the Millennium would be freedom from worship. It may be useful, as well, to declare independence from ghosts and other supernatural forces, as well as alien visitation. "The fault is not in our stars, but in ourselves."

A new ethic based on relationship emerges from the realization that human beings exist:

1. without "hope";
2. without new lives awaiting them;
3. without the prospect of restitution for loss;
4. without redemption for sin;
5. without an excuse for time wasted.

This means that the record of a person's conduct in this life is the entire record, that nothing will compensate us for our suffering, that we shall never find a paradise beyond this planet, and that there is no starting-over.

XV

What Is to be Done

What Is to be Done?
> —title of book by V. I. Lenin

Esdras (looking at the stars):
... in all these turning lights I find no clue, only a masterless night, and in my blood no certain answer, yet is my mind my own, yet is my heart a cry toward something dim in distance, which is higher than I am and makes me emperor of the endless dark even in seeking!
> —Maxwell Anderson, "Winterset"

Religion is an illusion and it derives its strength from its readiness to fit in with our instinctual wishful impulses.
> —Sigmund Freud,
> *New Introductory Lectures on Psycho-analysis*

135

Knowing the meaning of life, we can create a moral code that is grounded in the experience of mortal beings walking in a finite universe. If we are not going anywhere, we don't have to prepare for a journey. If we are not to be judged, we must judge ourselves. If we are not to be "saved," we must save ourselves. We are seeking an ethical philosophy that is practical for everyday life, but meets our need for spiritual gratification; it must be centered in the "here and now" and, above all, guide us through the hills and valleys of a life lived in and for relationships.

Formidable obstacles remain before us as we enter the Third Millennium, oppressive forces from an obsolete conception of life's purpose. These are noted here, in descending order of oppressiveness:

Religion
Nation
Race
Language
Culture

We can reason our way out of the grasp of each of these disabling influences by thinking along these lines—in ascending order of difficulty:

CULTURE[1]

A person's culture is the social environment into which one is born or in which one chooses to live, with its arbitrary rules and customs, prejudices and preferences, taboos and enthusiasms, art and cuisine. The tyranny of living in or being assimilated into a culture lies in the conceit that it differs significantly from the rest of the world's cultures; a worse conceit is that it is better than the others. The more one has traveled the world, the more one understands that people are the same everywhere, the same in every foible and in every worthwhile trait.

In short, the best thing to do about culture is to ignore it. It will go away eventually, of its own inconsequentiality. Its passing will be a blessing because having more than one culture keeps people apart, creating walls between one group and another in much the same way that languages do. If there were a single culture, the concept itself would disappear.

---

[1] "culture" (Webster): "The sum total of ways of living built up by a group of human beings and transmitted from one generation to another." The term is used here in this sense and not to refer to a person's aesthetic sensibilities, as when one says "She is a cultured woman."

LANGUAGE

Languages developed in tribes, and, in the never-ending conflict between and among tribes, languages served as a screening device to protect tribal security. If a stranger appeared who did not know the sounds that stand for water, he must have come from another tribe and be a possible menace. The Bible tells the story of the struggle between the Gileadites and the Ephraimites over Jordan: the men of Gilead had driven the men of Ephraim out, but when one of them tried to sneak back in, they said to him "Say now 'Shibboleth'; and he said 'Sibboleth', for he could not frame to pronounce it right," and the man was executed forthwith (Judges 12:6). Even today, an accent or a mistake of grammar or ill-chosen word reveals the outsider, who can be welcomed or scorned. Language drives a wedge between people and keeps prejudice alive. At this stage in civilization, a universal language is required.

RACE

The concept of race has bedeviled mankind forever, chiefly because tribal variations in physical characteristics helped to identify a potential enemy. No one disputes that basic differences in people are due to differing samples from the gene pool. Whether or not genes differ according to the attribute that we call "race" is debatable, and in fact some anthropologists view the concept as mythical; notable among them was Ashley Montagu, whose *Man's Most Dangerous Myth: The Fallacy of Race* is recognized as a classic on the subject.

As a "ruling fiction," race is oppressive because it fosters the belief that people differ significantly in aspects that are not susceptible to change. If there *are* races. nothing can be done about them short of intermarriage, and if there is only the human race the concept bears no weight. It emerges from the dark side, where anger dwells with its attendant negative emotions. Because it divides people, the malevolent force of race must be vanquished in this millennium.

NATION

A nation is an abstract entity, defined in most instances by tribe or race or religion or all three, separated from its neighbors by an artificial boundary such as a river or mountain range. No one but a radical chauvinist believes that a nation is endowed by a god, or that a person's national origin is anything but a happenstance of time and place. The notion that a child of American parents who is born in Iran should be an Iranian citizen shows national pride at its most absurd and xenophobia at its most extreme.

The times are changing. Recently, the French political scholar Bernard-Henri Lévy wrote that " . . . we have overcome romantic nationalism." He alluded to the European Union, a collaboration producing the world's strongest economy, a reality that reveals the obsolescence of nations.

Nationhood spawns wars and wars destroy relationships. Therefore, nations are evil. They serve no useful purpose.

RELIGION

Organized religion operates by means of the power of suggestion, in which one is persuaded to believe what one most wishes to believe, such as "God loves me" or "I am promised eternal life." The same persuasive power is the operative principle in brainwashing. Religion is not the opium of the people, as Karl Marx would have it, but its hypnotic spell.

People fell prey to this oppression by means of a process like this: the ultimate human striving—life after death—led us to the concept of a being more powerful than death. The Pharaohs had this power in one chapter of the human comedy, and then came Jehovah and Allah and the rest of the gods, each of whom asked obedience in exchange for salvation.

Why is religion so dangerous to us? Because, in its every guise and manifestation, in every thought that it provokes, it is oriented to death. Imagine that, if it were not for dying, religion would have no appeal. To live forever would make religion irrelevant, and if each day of life were perfect, the idea of a religion would never occur to us. Reversing this sequence of thinking, if we concentrated on our finite lives, we might be able to enjoy them more fully. The secret of life is living it—not the next life but this one.

I am saddened when I see pictures of Christian and Muslim people kneeling and bowing down their bodies in prayer.[1] They humble themselves because of superstition or fantasy or self-delusion. In this pose, they appear to me as a different species, forsaking their real relationships in the here-and-now, for a relationship with a god that cannot exist and a wish that can never come true. There will be no Deliverance and no Rapture will lift them into the sky. They live these moments alone, and cannot see that the persons kneeling beside them hold the keys to their salvation. Stand up, look around you, and *relate*.

Imagine a world without the sorcery of religion, without the alienation of national boundaries, in which cultural differences are colorful but irrelevant (none better than any other), and in which there are no races and one language. This world will come.

---

[1]   I feel the same way about Jews at the Wailing Wall in their stupid hats, or Buddhists chanting "Om." It's *supplication* that demeans the human spirit.

XVI

A Philosopher's Agenda

Philosophy is human thought become self-conscious.
Its topics are life, the universe, and everything; it
can include all the categories of religious, artistic,
scientific, mathematical, and logical thought.

—Simon Blackburn,
The Oxford Dictionary of Philosophy

One can only admire the pretension—and pity the futility—of Philosophy as defined above. Perhaps it was foolish to expect much insight into religion, art, science, or mathematics from a gadfly on the rump of those other disciplines. The fact is that not since the Nineteenth Century have we been able to learn much about life from Philosophy. Its failure to confront the major issues is a sad chronicle of intellectual poverty in our time.

The burning questions of the Third Millennium will not be answered by biochemists, astronauts, poets, engineers, politicians, clergymen, or doctors of medicine, nor by butchers, bakers, or candlestick-makers. Even so, those who do provide the answers will be philosophers, and philosophers who evade those questions should give their robes to charity. (Some of the questions that they have ignored were noted in Chapter XI.) What held them back is an antiquated view of human nature, according to which people exist to pass a test, prove themselves, leave a legacy, or "make a difference." In this view, life is preparation, a trial, an ordeal, a "pilot" for the drama that will be staged at some other time in some other medium for an audience yet to be invited to attend; this life is no more than a shadow-play of the apotheosis to come. As Alexander Pope put it, "Man never is, but always to-be blessed."

Now that we have a clear conception of the meaning of life in mind, we can apply the criterion of relationship to a few "knotty problems," which are knotty only because we have approached them from a clouded perspective.

These include questions such as "When does life begin?" and "When does life end?"

WHEN LIFE BEGINS

Whether life begins at the moment of birth or the moment of conception is a subject of unceasing debate. That debate lacks the key reference-point of life's *meaning*. If life is relationship. the instant when life begins is when the first relationship is formed. This happens at birth, when the mother first holds the newborn in her arms. Some people would say that the relationship starts when the child is in the womb, but that is metaphor: it uses the term "relationship" in a way that it was not meant to be used. We might as well say that a person forms a relationship with his or her heart or, if one has a tumor, with the tumor. It's understood that relationship requires some kind of communication between those who relate to each-other, and that this process of interaction between mother and child begins at birth. A non-verbal communication it is, but it involves the exchange of messages and certainly qualifies as a first step in the formation of a bond between them.

In the same way that relationship defines the meaning of life, it marks the birth of identity. In the womb, the child lacks personhood. A sense of self waits upon the awareness of other selves, a revelation that occurs when his or her eyes first open to the sight of the mother-figure. *To exist means being in a relationship*. Therefore, relationship precedes existence.

WHEN LIFE ENDS

To this philosophical problem can be applied similar reasoning. If life is relationship, life ends when the last relationship ends. As the final hour approaches, the average person has three or four valued relationships that provide him or her with comfort and reassurance. As darkness closes in, the relationship at hand becomes the most cherished of all; as the saying goes, "Let every lover be the last." When it is no longer possible for two people to communicate, there can be no relationship. When no relationship is possible, there is no reason for living.

If euthanasia is an issue, it is certainly not necessary for a doctor or nurse or hospital administrator (or even a philosopher) to decide when life support should be withdrawn. This decision should rest with the last relationship partner, who will have concluded that communication has ceased. Naturally, the person who is dying will have an opinion that must be respected, in answer to the question "Who should end your life when the time comes?" The timing of the decision is left to the survivor of this final relationship, to the last best person in one's life.

From the womb to the grave, Philosophy can identify issues that people can explore for themselves, to make their lives more meaningful. Examples include:

- What was the love of your life?
- Will you fall in love again?

- What will you never do?
- Where will you never go?
- Will you live to attend the wedding of your grandchild?
- What message do you plan to leave to your grandchildren?
- Where will you die?
- What illness or injury might kill you?
- What time of your life was the best?
- What should people do to honor your memory?

Subjects such as these are intensely personal, and not everyone would find them relevant; moreover, they would only be relevant at certain stages of a person's life and not before. Regardless of when it occurs, this inquiry takes its purpose from Socrates' "The unexamined life is not worth living" (as quoted by Plato, his pupil). The task of the philosopher is to set this examination, to remind people of the questions that are worth asking of themselves.

XVII

The First Relationship

The love of a mother for her child is the basic patent and model for all human relationships . . . It is the way of love in which human beings may live most successfully and happily and in optimum health, and it is the evolutionary destiny of human beings so to love each other. I believe it is the unique function and destiny of women to teach humankind to live as if to live and love were one.

—Ashley Montagu,
The Natural Superiority of Women

The purest relationship given to mankind is the one between mother and child. When a woman gives birth to a child, the emotional and spiritual bond that forms between them is as deep and lasting as any in human experience. This relationship is saintly, without blemish or complaint. It is all-consuming, unrestrained by modesty or self-consciousness. Mother and child give themselves to each-other as they would to themselves. What singleness of purpose that began in the womb resumes immediately after the cataclysm of birthing has torn them apart. What had been one organism is reunited with itself. Being born and having given birth are life's only transcendencies. Their magic no one can explain.

Every other form of relationship pales by comparison with that of mother and child. When becoming a mother for the first time, a woman summons abilities and traits acquired long ago, of course, from her own mother and as practiced with her dolls. These traits include tenderness, compassion, patience, forgiveness, and an attentiveness seldom muted by sleep. In their earliest studies, researchers into the dynamics of non-verbal behavior identified a phenomenon that they called "direction of gaze." This is a vital component of beneficial interaction between mother and infant, in which the mother directs her gaze constantly toward the child, enabling the child to make eye contact whenever it needs reassurance. This *regard* for the child and receptivity to the child's feelings and needs is what a healthy mother-child connection requires. Should the mother often avert her gaze or break the connection repeatedly and without warning, trouble may lie ahead for the child. In fact, some have implicated the mother's turning away and witholding of eye contact as a causal factor in the development of infantile autism, a severe psychiatric disorder.

So the good mother gives of herself by offering her regard, and the child thrives as a result. In her turn, the mother sees the child returning her gaze, and knows that she is the center of the child's world. She knows, as well, that she is a proper mother. In their hermetic world, they share their essences. Here is a form of symbiosis of which Nature approves.

The oneness of mother and child is a oneness not of Being but of two earthbound spirits, and it becomes the prototype for every relationship worthy of the name. The first relationship is the model of those that follow. Interaction begins here, without words; its sole active ingredient is the *connection* between two people—expressed by looks and touches and sounds. With each interaction, life becomes more meaningful for both participants, because by living for each-other, they fulfill themselves. Few partners, no more than a few times in life, experience closeness of this intensity.[1]

The Life Force, normally exerting its influence on creatures subtly and symbolically, provides us with a

---

[1]   Those horrendous instances when children have not been cared-for, or have even been harmed by their mothers, are truly crimes against Nature.

powerful lesson just as our lives begin: the newborn and the mother learn to share and to benefit from sharing. The child takes affection from its mother and, if the mother is able to nurse, nurturance. By suckling the child at her breast, a mother can herself be nurtured by the very hormonal system that makes lactating possible. This primordial interdependence is the wellspring of the child's development and a rich source of the mother's fulfillment through motherhood. If it is true that a woman is not entirely fulfilled until she has given birth, it is equally true that a person's experience of being mothered presages one's future experience of relationship.[1] Being mothered, for example, teaches empathy, a beatific state in which one person intuits what another person is feeling.

An empathetic sensibility is made, not born; it requires:

---

[1] The biological mother with her newborn is the most complete, reciprocal expression of bonding. To be sure, fathers bond with their newborn children. The intensity of their affinity may not be as great as that between mother and child, but surely it is qualitatively the same. The deficiencies of fatherhood, in which the physical connection is at several removes, are well known. Even so, father and child can relate to each-other in many ways, both emotionally and psychologically. The developmental stages of this growing-together were meticulously explored in Martin Greenberg's delightful book, *The Birth of a Father*. Of course, a child can experience having a surrogate mother or father with whom he or she relates just as intimately as with a biological parent.

1. a parent who asks about, and expresses concern for, how the child is feeling on frequent occasions;
2. a parent who tells the child, honestly, how he or she is feeling about significant events in his or her life;
3. a parent who discusses, with the child, both the parent's and the child's observations of how other persons are feeling.

The ability to empathize can be learned by the tenth year of life and remains a lifelong trait. It is noticeably missing in psychopaths, sociopaths, and sadists of any stripe. When present, it will leaven and enlighten any disagreement between people, because it shows a willingness, as they say, to wear the other person's shoes and see life through another's eyes. Here is the Golden Rule in practical terms. An emphatic bond is the finest expression of relationship.

Note that this blueprint of what to expect of a relationship, based on the mother-child interaction, is of two people meeting each-other's needs. Nature has paired them, for a purpose we may never comprehend but nonetheless compelling by its universality. "We are meant to live for others," wrote Camus, and each person's entry into the world affirms that destiny. Duality precedes individuality.

POSTSCRIPT

Man, that is born of a woman, hath but a short time
to live, and is full of misery. He cometh up, and is
cut down, like a flower; he fleeth as it were a shadow,
and never continueth in one stay. In the midst of
life we are in death.

—"Burial of the Dead,"
in *The Book of Common Prayer*

The patterns of life encompass relationship, from its finest flowering in maternity to its degradation by suicide. A life is wasted because a relationship has failed; or, a life is sustained and fulfilled by relationship. It can make us crazy and it can inspire in us undying love. We enter life from a dark place into light, and with our first breaths we relate to others without hesitation, drawn to them by the same force that seeks survival. Relationship tells you when to start living and when it's time to die. It is not just a way of life. It is life.

INDEX

C

Calvin, John 78
Cambridge University Press 11
Campbell, Joseph *(The Power of Myth)* 33
Camus, Albert 25, 26, 36, 52, 57, 87, 89, 93, 95, 118, 153
"Caligula" 95
L'Étranger 93
poet of indifference 87
The Myth of Sisyphus 25, 52
Candide 85
Casebook on Existentialism, A (Spanos) 40
Catch-22 (Heller) 45
Chain of Being 94
Chekhov, Anton 99, 131
The Three Sisters 131
Uncle Vanya 99
chemistry 64
Ch'in Dynasty 128
Choir Celestial 100
Cocktail Party, The (Eliot) 105
Cogito, ergo sum 38
collective unconscious 62
communal autism 113
communication 64
complementarity 69
compromise 68, 69
conceit 90
Conceptions of Modern Psychiatry (Sullivan) 41, 46, 51
confession 90

connection 151
contents of consciousness 121
Cosmic Plan 62
Coward, Noel 65
culture 34, 137
Cult of the Self 48
curtain call 101

D

Dalai Lama 121
Dante 76, 108, 117
Death of a Salesman 89
deceit 81, 82
Deliverance 141
Descartes, Rene *(Discourse on Method)* 38
Desdemona 81
desire 65
destiny 92, 133
direction of gaze 150
Discourse on Method (Descartes) 38
Divine Providence 90
DNA 21
Dostoevsky, Fyodor 109
"double bind, the" 45
Dreiser, Theodore *(Sister Carrie)* 75
duality 153

E

Edmonds *(Wittgenstein's Poker)* 12
Eidinow *(Wittgenstein's Poker)* 12
Einstein, Albert 38
Eliot, T. S. 105, 106